## Early praise for *Deliver Audacious Web Apps with Ember 2*

*Deliver Audacious Web Apps with Ember 2* provides a clear and thorough introduction to the powerful and elegant Ember framework. Developers looking to learn Ember or level up their Ember skills should read this book.

➤ **Nell Shamrell-Harrington**
  Software development engineer, Chef

Ember brought back the fun of Rails, this time for single-page applications with great performance.

➤ **Federico Tomassetti**
  Software engineer

If you're considering Ember for your next JavaScript project, buy this book. I felt like I'd leveled up after every chapter.

➤ **Stephen Orr**
  Senior software engineer, Impact Applications

Many of the designations used by manufacturers and sellers to distinguish their products are claimed as trademarks. Where those designations appear in this book, and The Pragmatic Programmers, LLC was aware of a trademark claim, the designations have been printed in initial capital letters or in all capitals. The Pragmatic Starter Kit, The Pragmatic Programmer, Pragmatic Programming, Pragmatic Bookshelf, PragProg and the linking *g* device are trademarks of The Pragmatic Programmers, LLC.

Every precaution was taken in the preparation of this book. However, the publisher assumes no responsibility for errors or omissions, or for damages that may result from the use of information (including program listings) contained herein.

Our Pragmatic courses, workshops, and other products can help you and your team create better software and have more fun. For more information, as well as the latest Pragmatic titles, please visit us at *https://pragprog.com*.

The team that produced this book includes:

Katharine Dvorak (editor)
Potomac Indexing, LLC (index)
Liz Welch (copyedit)
Dave Thomas (layout)
Janet Furlow (producer)
Ellie Callahan (support)

For international rights, please contact *rights@pragprog.com*.

Printed in the United States of America.
ISBN-13: 978-1-68050-078-3
Printed on acid-free paper.
Book version: P1.0—October 2015

# Deliver Audacious Web Apps
# with Ember 2

Matthew White

The Pragmatic Bookshelf

Dallas, Texas • Raleigh, North Carolina

# Contents

Acknowledgments . . . . . . . . . . . . vii

Introduction: Why Ember? . . . . . . . . . . ix

1.   **Starting Your App with Ember** . . . . . . . . 1

     Install Ember and Ember CLI          1

     Start Your App          3

     Next Steps          16

2.   **Directing Traffic with Routes** . . . . . . . . 17

     Use the Router Class to Organize Your App     17

     Define Your Routes     19

     Set Your Model     23

     Nest Routes     30

     Transition Between Routes     32

     Render Templates into Named Outlets     33

     Next Steps     34

3.   **Laying Out a User Interface** . . . . . . . . . 35

     Make Your App with a Single Page     35

     Segment Your UI into Templates     38

     Render HTML Controls with Expressions     41

     Compile Templates     46

     Next Steps     47

4.   **Building In Reuse with Components** . . . . . . . 49

     Create Components     50

     Get Data from Containing Templates     52

     Define a Component User Interface     53

     Handle Actions     57

     Next Steps     61

| 5. | **Modeling Your Data** . . . . . . . . . . . | **63** |
|---|---|---|
| | Define Your Models | 63 |
| | Load Data from RESTful Services | 65 |
| | Work with Records | 70 |
| | Next Steps | 76 |

| 6. | **Reading Nonstandard APIs** . . . . . . . . . | **77** |
|---|---|---|
| | Adapt to a Nonconventional API | 77 |
| | Use Serializers to Access Legacy APIs | 82 |
| | Allow the Adapter to Query a Nonconventional API | 85 |
| | Adapt to Path Name Variations | 86 |
| | Change the Payload Root | 86 |
| | Modify the Payload in Flight | 87 |
| | Tie Adapters and Serializers to Your Model Class | 89 |
| | Next Steps | 89 |

| 7. | **Reusing Code in Ember** . . . . . . . . . | **91** |
|---|---|---|
| | Abstract Common Functions with Utilities | 91 |
| | Share Code with Mixins | 94 |
| | Share Services with Dependency Injection | 98 |
| | Use Transforms to Tweak Data | 102 |
| | Next Steps | 104 |

| 8. | **Building, Testing, and Deploying Your Ember Apps** . . . | **105** |
|---|---|---|
| | Build Your App | 105 |
| | Test and Debug Your App | 107 |
| | Deploy Your App | 119 |
| | Next Steps | 119 |

| 9. | **Building and Using Ember Addons** . . . . . . . | **121** |
|---|---|---|
| | Install an Ember Addon | 121 |
| | Develop Your Own Addon | 122 |
| | Next Steps | 129 |

| | **Index** . . . . . . . . . . . . . | **131** |
|---|---|---|

# Acknowledgments

Every book is the result of a lot of behind-the-scenes effort, particularly if that book was written by a first-time author. The following people were very helpful to me in creating this book.

To the Ember core team and the Ember community: Thank you for making a product that was fun to learn and to write about. The web is better off because you volunteered your time. Thank you!

To my technical reviewers, Alessandro Bahgat, Jacob Chae, Javier Collado, Jeremy Frens, Kenneth Geisshirt, Alexander Henry, Eric Hung, Jan Nonnen, Stephen Orr, Shreerang Patwardhan, Martijn Reuvers, Brian Schau, Nell Shamrell-Harrington, Tibor Simic, Charley Stran, Federico Tomassetti, Paul Waring, Nick Watts, and Stephen Wolff: Thank you for lending your time and expertise to this project. Your comments made this a much better book than I would have written alone.

To The Pragmatic Bookshelf, including Andy Hunt, Dave Thomas, Susannah Davidson Pfalzer, Janet Furlow, and anyone else who had a hand in production: You helped me shape this into something I hope we can all be proud to have our names on.

To my editor, Katharine Dvorak: This is as much your book as mine. Your guidance and vision were so helpful to me, and without them, this book would be twice as long with half as much useful information. I can't wait to start on the next book!

To my good friend and fellow author, Sharone Williams: Thank you for commiserating with me over deadline-induced delusions. It was immeasurably helpful knowing you were also out there in the word mines.

To my parents: Thank you for all the sacrifices you made for me, and for teaching me to work hard and try new things. I hope you're as proud of this book as I am.

Most important, to my wife and son: Your patience, support, and love mean everything to me, and I would have neither started nor finished this book without you. Thank you for everything!

**Matt White**

matt@mattwhite.co

October, 2015

# Introduction: Why Ember?

When you think about writing a web app, what excites you most? Do you look forward to writing framework code, or delivering features to your users? If you're like me, the features are the exciting stuff, and the framework exists to serve the features. Now, imagine if a group of developers had gone looking for best practices in creating a web app front end, and then codified what they found into a framework. Imagine if instead of worrying about writing glue code, you could spend your time on the exciting stuff. How would your work be different?

Ember is an open source JavaScript framework, maintained at emberjs.com and on GitHub,[1] that speeds the development of web apps. It provides much of the front-end infrastructure you need so that you can spend your time making a great app. If you use Ember, you'll write less code and you'll write simpler code. And simpler code is better code. By injecting object-oriented design principles into JavaScript to help you structure your code in a sensible way, Ember lets you think at a modular level. This makes your app easier to create and to maintain.

In this book, you'll learn how to create audacious web apps and do so efficiently by letting Ember do the heavy lifting. You'll use Ember's routing system to build single-page apps with rich interfaces and simple, shareable URLs. You'll create reusable UI components and templates and compose them into highly usable, sophisticated apps. You'll use Ember Data to read and write to RESTful services. You'll learn to use Ember addons to share code and use code others have shared. And you'll learn to use Ember CLI and QUnit to organize, build, and test your apps.

---

1.   github.com/emberjs/ember.js/

## What This Book Is, and Isn't

This book is a brisk introduction to the core features of Ember 2, Ember Data, and Ember CLI. These features rely on Node.js, npm, and Handlebars, but we won't go into detail on these dependencies.

This book is not an exhaustive reference on Ember, Ember Data, or Ember CLI. I hope you'll learn enough to pique your curiosity, but we won't cover every last Ember API. This book is also not an introduction to JavaScript or to web development. I assume you have some knowledge of JavaScript, DOM, Ajax, HTML/CSS, and RESTful services.

## Who Should Read This Book?

This book is intended for web developers who are new to Ember. If you've used other frameworks such as React or AngularJS, or if you've used jQuery, some of the ideas behind Ember should be familiar to you, but if not, you should be fine.

## How This Book Is Organized

In the first chapter, we'll begin by creating our local development environment, and then start working on a sample project. We'll briefly touch on many of the core features in this first chapter while we build a small, but complete, example feature.

In the next three chapters, we'll focus on the core aspects of building a user interface with Ember 2, and see how it uses routes, templates, and components to dynamically keep your interface up to date without a lot of clunky round-trips to the server. In Chapters 5 and 6, we concentrate on using models with Ember Data to access a RESTful service to obtain data and provide that data to the user interface. Chapter 7 discusses a few ways to promote code reuse within your Ember app, including utilities, mixins, and dependency injection. And we'll finish up in Chapters 8 and 9 by learning how to use Ember CLI for building, testing, and deploying apps, as well as sharing code through addons.

One thing that's a little different about this book is that each chapter builds on the work done in a previous chapter. We will work together to build a single app, starting on page one, and continuing throughout. For that reason, it's best if you read the book in order on your first pass through. Once you've read through the book, then you'll have better luck using it as a reference, but it works best as a progressive tutorial on your first read.

Together, we'll build an app called EmberNote. It's a simplified clone of the Evernote app, which is a web-based notetaking application. Using Evernote as a model, we'll use Evernote's hierarchical structure of notebooks and notes to learn how to use Ember's routing system and Ember Data's data access library. We'll build a Markdown-driven edit tool to help us prepare HTML-formatted notes, and learn about Ember's component feature in the process. We'll learn how to use Ember CLI to build, test, deploy, and share cool code from our app. Last, throughout the book, we'll learn how to use Ember CLI addons to add cool features to our app, such as authentication and component libraries.

## Where to Go for Help

All of the coding examples in this book can be found online on the book's web page.[2] There you will also find a discussion forum where you can ask questions and provide feedback.

Now, let's get started!

---

2. pragprog.com/book/mwjsember

# CHAPTER 1

# Starting Your App with Ember

In this chapter, we'll get off to a running start by learning some of the core features of Ember and Ember CLI. First, we'll set up our development environment by installing Ember and Ember CLI. Next, we'll start building the app that we'll work on throughout this book. We'll use Ember CLI to create the app and its first feature: a registration page. Finally, we'll back up this page by building a basic, data-aware back end for testing purposes. Let's get started by installing Ember and Ember CLI.

## Install Ember and Ember CLI

Ember CLI is a command-line interface for building Ember apps, and it's the project team's preferred means of obtaining the framework libraries. In general, Ember is heavily focused on what the Ember developers call "developer ergonomics." They want to make your life as a developer easier. Ember CLI was created in that spirit. As you'll see throughout the book, Ember CLI makes short work out of a lot of boilerplate tasks, such as building and deploying, executing tests, adding files to create new features, and so on. Equally important, it allows you to use a new module-based syntax for your classes. This adds greatly to the clarity of your code. We'll use Ember CLI throughout this book, so let's get started by installing it.

Ember CLI has a few prerequisites: Node, Bower, and PhantomJS. Ember CLI relies on Node to provide a JavaScript environment outside of your browser. It uses Bower for help with dependency management. And it uses PhantomJS as a test execution environment.

It's worth noting that while we'll use Node to run the Ember CLI development tools, Ember itself isn't a server-side framework, despite the fact that Node supports server-side JavaScript development. Ember is used for creating browser-resident apps.

To begin, let's install Node[1] and npm,[2] as well as Git.[3] Node comes with npm, but npm is updated frequently, so it's worth confirming that you have the latest. Please visit the sites to install the most recent version of these tools for your particular platform. Your Node install should be at least version 0.12 to support Ember CLI tooling. If you already have Node installed, you may need to uninstall the existing version first.

The latter two installs are required by Bower. Npm is a package manager for code built to run within Node, or to be used with a tool that runs in Node. Git is a distributed version control system. Install all three using the installation instructions at the respective sites.

---

**Installation**

When installing each of these tools, you'll want to be running as an administrative user. On a Linux/BSD/OS X system, you'll probably want to use the sudo prefix to do this, and on Windows, you'll need to be signed in as a user with admin rights. As with many installations, there are things that can go wrong, so if an issue arises, head to the book's forum on pragprog.com and we'll work through it together.

---

With these tools installed, you can get Bower from a command line:

```
$ npm install -g bower
```

You should see several lines of command output, indicating that Bower and its dependencies have been pulled onto your machine. The -g command option asks Node to install Bower and make it available globally, rather than restricting it to a specific project. Once Bower has finished installing (you'll see the command output stop and be returned to the command prompt), you can install PhantomJS:

```
$ npm install -g phantomjs
```

Again, you should see some command output that tells you PhantomJS was installed successfully. With these tools, you're ready to get Ember CLI:

```
$ npm install -g ember-cli
```

Installing Ember CLI causes the Ember framework libraries to be installed, along with the CLI itself. Now that you have Ember and Ember CLI, we're ready to start coding.

---

1.    nodejs.org
2.    npmjs.com
3.    git-scm.com/downloads

# Start Your App

Ember CLI takes a very app-centric approach. The first thing you do is to create the app, and every module you create is part of that app. As a result, we're going to follow suit, and explore all of Ember's key concepts in the context of one app.

We'll be writing an app called EmberNote, a slimmed-down clone of Evernote,[4] the web-based note-taking app. Our first step is to create the app's repository (so called because Ember CLI assumes you'll be using Git as a version control system).

## Creating the App Repository

Open a command prompt, navigate to a location where you keep your code, and run the following command:

```
$ ember new ember-note
```

This will create a new directory for your app. Take a look at the tip that follows if any issues arise.

**New Projects with Ember CLI**

As of this writing, there's a probable race condition that can occur with Ember CLI when creating a new repository. If you see an error that looks something like this: ENOENT, open 'ember/package.json', you may have run into this error. Usually, the ember new command succeeds on the second try.

On certain non-Windows systems, you may also see a console warning about not having watchman installed. Ember CLI uses watchman to monitor your filesystem for changes and live deploys them to your local server as you're working on your Ember app. It's good to have watchman, if for no other reason than to avoid seeing this error, but it's not necessary. Without watchman, Ember CLI uses a tool called NodeWatcher for the same purpose. If you want to install watchman, visit facebook.github.io/watchman/docs/install.html for platform-specific installation instructions.

Before we write our UI code, let's also install a Bootstrap stylesheet so we can enjoy a UI that doesn't look like it's from the early 1990s. From a command prompt in the newly created ember-note directory, run the following commands:

---

4. evernote.com

```
$ cd ember-note
$ npm install
$ bower install
$ bower install bootstrap --save
```

Then add these lines to ember-note/ember-cli-build.js, right before the last line of code:

```
app.import('bower_components/bootstrap/dist/css/bootstrap.css');
app.import('bower_components/bootstrap/dist/css/bootstrap.css.map',{
  destDir: 'assets'
});
```

When you run these commands, Ember CLI creates your app's folder structure for you. Our task throughout the rest of this book is to take that structure and fill in all of the details to make an app out of it. Make no mistake, Ember and Ember CLI are opinionated tools. They have built-in expectations of how to develop web apps, known as *convention-over-configuration*. The Ember team hopes to take a set of best practices, codify them into the framework, and allow the developer to focus on more important decisions. To get good use from these tools, you'll want to follow their lead.

## Running Your App

Let's run the app we made and see what that looks like. From a command prompt in your new ember-note directory, run the following command:

```
$ ember serve
```

You should see some command output that tells you that your build was successful and that your app is running on port 4200 of your localhost. Let's open the browser and check. You should see something similar to the output shown in the following figure if you point your browser to localhost:4200.

The ember serve command did a few things for you. First, it built a deployable version of your app and placed it in the ember-note/dist directory. Then, it started a node instance at port 4200 and deployed your app to that instance for testing. Once you've run this command, it will pick up on changes you make to the source code.

Let's try one now. Open the ember-note/app/templates/application.hbs file. Its contents should look like this:

```
<h2 id="title">Welcome to Ember</h2>

{{outlet}}
```

Make a change to the file so the text says "Welcome to EmberNote." The file should then look like this:

```
<h2 id="title">Welcome to EmberNote</h2>

{{outlet}}
```

As soon as you save the change, look at your browser. Ember CLI detected the change, rebuilt your app, and deployed it when you saved. This is a big time-saver, because you don't have to manually take steps to redeploy the app yourself. It all happens out of the box with Ember CLI!

You can see that Ember CLI is a handy tool to have around. Now it's time to get into some code. If we're going to build an app, we'll need to be able to let users sign up, right? Let's start there.

## Registering Users

Let's look at a straightforward example that will demonstrate many of the core features of an Ember app: routes, templates, and models. We're going to build a simplified registration page that will allow users to sign up for the EmberNote service. This page has a single text field where the user can enter his or her username, a button to trigger the add action, and some text that will be displayed when a new user is added.

In an Ember app, all of your functionality is organized under routes. A *route* is in essence a URL segment, as described in *Nest Routes*, on page 30. So, our next step is to use Ember CLI to create a route. Open a new command shell, and from the root of your ember-note project, run the following command:

```
$ ember generate route register --pod
```

The --pod flag, when added to the generate command, creates a directory called register, which includes the files that are needed to add your route: route.js and template.hbs. They are empty at the moment, and you'll fill them out as needed to create the route's features. Generally speaking, you use a pod when you want to organize your project by feature (that is, create a register directory with a route.js and a template.hbs file), rather than by object type.

Earlier, when you created the app with the ember new command, the following four files were created: index.html, app.js, router.js, and application.hbs. The ember generate command then edits the router.js file under your app directory. We'll dig into this more in *Use the Router Class to Organize Your App*, on page 17, but the router.js class is used to implement the hierarchy of routes within your application.

If you run the ember generate command but leave off the --pod flag, Ember CLI still creates the same objects, but instead of creating a file called route.js in the register directory, it creates a file called register.js in the route directory. For our purposes, it's preferable to see each of the files we need for a route in one location, so we'll use the --pod flag throughout the book.

Let's take a look at each of the files we've created so far.

### index.html

This file is the starting point for your application. It was created when you ran the ember new ember-note command. Let's have a look.

```
ch1/ember-note/app/index.html
<!DOCTYPE html>
<html>
  <head>
    <meta charset="utf-8">
    <meta http-equiv="X-UA-Compatible" content="IE=edge">
    <title>EmberNote</title>
    <meta name="description" content="">
    <meta name="viewport" content="width=device-width, initial-scale=1">

    {{content-for 'head'}}

    <link rel="stylesheet" href="assets/vendor.css">
    <link rel="stylesheet" href="assets/ember-note.css">

    {{content-for 'head-footer'}}
  </head>
  <body>
    {{content-for 'body'}}

    <script src="assets/vendor.js"></script>
    <script src="assets/ember-note.js"></script>

    {{content-for 'body-footer'}}
  </body>
</html>
```

The majority of index.html is boilerplate HTML to create a starting page. Ember CLI adds in two stylesheets named vendor.css and ember-note.css to style the application. We won't be doing much with stylesheets in this book, but you should know that vendor.css will capture styles used in any third-party code you bring into the app, and ember-note.css is for styles that you define.

The same thing applies to vendor.js and ember-note.js. The Ember CLI build process creates one file for all of the third-party code you use in your app, called vendor.js, and one for your application code, called ember-note.js. These are included in index.html.

You may also notice the {{content-for}} expressions. These allow you to include additional content in your page using Ember CLI addons.

### app.js

The app.js file is used to create the Ember environment. Take a look at the following code:

```
ch1/ember-note/app/app.js
import Ember from 'ember';
import Resolver from 'ember/resolver';
import loadInitializers from 'ember/load-initializers';
import config from './config/environment';

var App;

Ember.MODEL_FACTORY_INJECTIONS = true;

App = Ember.Application.extend({
  modulePrefix: config.modulePrefix,
  podModulePrefix: config.podModulePrefix,
  Resolver: Resolver
});

loadInitializers(App, config.modulePrefix);

export default App;
```

If you're a veteran JavaScript developer who hasn't looked at ECMAScript 2015 yet, the first four lines may have your eyes popping out of your head. ECMAScript is the formal name of the JavaScript language as specified by ECMA International, and ECMAScript 2015 (also known as ECMAScript 6 or ES6) is the latest release of the standard. Yes, those four lines are importing dependencies from other JavaScript files to use their modules within the current module. This is a hugely important aspect of using Ember CLI. When you start writing your code in a modular fashion, your dependencies become easier to reason about, and you eliminate the need to stuff objects into the global scope. It also helps you to structure your code in a way that makes sense. Don't worry whether the browser supports ECMAScript 2015, though. Ember CLI transpiles your code into a format that the browser can execute.

The purpose of the code in app.js is to set up app-wide constructs. One of these, the Ember Resolver, is used to look up classes throughout the app. The modulePrefix variable is set to the value ember-note, as defined when you set up your app. The podModulePrefix isn't set, as it wasn't defined yet for our project configuration, which was read from config/environment.js.

The last line of the file makes the App class available as a module. Don't worry if this doesn't quite make sense yet—you'll see many more examples of how Ember modules work as we go along. For now, let's look at another file that was created when the app was set up, the router.js file.

### router.js

The router.js file is where you can really start to see how Ember works. One of the most fundamental features of Ember is the notion of a route. Simply put, a route is a location within your app. If you think of your app as a collection of pages or page sections, each nested within one another, then each of those pages corresponds to a route. And the Router class, as defined in router.js, is where you define the structure of your app. Let's look at the code:

`ch1/ember-note/app/router.js`

```
import Ember from 'ember';
import config from './config/environment';

var Router = Ember.Router.extend({
  location: config.locationType
});

Router.map(function() {
  this.route('register');
});

export default Router;
```

At the top of the router.js file you see the necessary imports. In the class definition, which begins with var Router = Ember.Router.extend, we're bringing in some configuration variables from the global configuration as defined when we set up the app.

But Router.map is where the real action happens. As you can see, we've already created a route called register. This route was added to the Router when we ran the ember generate route register --pod command. A number of other files were also generated, and we'll edit those files to create our registration feature in a moment. The register route appears to be a top-level route, but is actually at the first level of child routes beneath a default route for the application. Let's look at that default route by way of its associated template.

### application.hbs

Each application has a root route, the Application route. Further, each route corresponds to exactly one template. A template is a chunk of your user interface. In the case of the application route, this template is defined in application.hbs. Let's modify this template now to look like the following:

```
ch1/ember-note/app/templates/application.hbs
<div class="container">
  <div class="row">
    <div class="col-md-2">
      Welcome to EmberNote
    </div>
    <div class="col-md-10">
      {{#link-to 'register'}}register{{/link-to}}
    </div>
  </div>
  <div class="row">
    <div>
      {{outlet}}
    </div>
  </div>
</div>
```

Each Ember template is a mixture of HTML and the Handlebars expression language, which is the portions of code set off with "{{ }}" characters. Handlebars is an expression language used by Ember to describe those segments of Ember templates that are in some way related to the Ember application code. You'll see many examples of Ember using Handlebars expressions throughout the book, always using the "{{ }}" characters. Ember ships with a compiler that turns Handlebars template expressions into DOM objects, as we'll see in *Compile Templates*, on page 46.

As we saw earlier, each app consists of a hierarchy of routes. The {{#link-to}} expression in the application.hbs file is used to generate a hyperlink that when clicked will load the register route into the {{outlet}}.

You may be wondering where the Application route is defined. In this particular case, because we don't have any specific action handling or data loading to do, we don't need to define the route class; we can simply rely on Ember to create a route implementation on the fly using default route behavior.

All of the code we've seen thus far has set up the bare minimum of application. Now, let's see how to add a feature to our app by building our register route.

## Building the Register Route

As discussed earlier, the register route will allow a user to register for the EmberNote app by choosing a username. When we created this route using the CLI, the following file was created (note, this is route.js, which is different from router.js):

```
ch1/ember-note/app/register/route.js
import Ember from 'ember';

export default Ember.Route.extend({
});
```

This is how you define an empty route class. A route has two primary reasons to exist: loading data to be displayed by the route and responding to actions. In our case, we don't have any data to display, and we need to define an addNew action to add new users to the app. We'll come back to that action shortly. First, let's see what the user interface will look like. Here's our route's template file, with the necessary UI code added in:

```
ch1/ember-note/app/register/template.hbs
<div class="col-md-12">
  Register new user: {{input value=name}}
  <button {{action 'addNew'}}>Add</button>
</div>
<div class="col-md-12">
  {{message}}
</div>
```

The {{input}} field allows us to key in a name, which will be added to the name attribute of the controller (which we'll create in a moment). The {{action}} expression, which we included in the <button>, binds the button's click action to the addNew action in our route. And the {{message}} expression simply displays the contents of the message attribute in the controller. We don't yet have a child route for register, but if we did, it would be rendered into {{outlet}}, similar to how the register route is rendered into the {{outlet}} in application.hbs.

We'll need some way to capture the UI state contained in the name and message fields. To do this, we'll rely on the default controller. In Ember, each route maps to exactly one controller, and that controller acts as a proxy for the underlying model, including any UI state. Because we don't have any data to load into our model yet, all we really use the controller for is to provide a place to put the state of the name and message fields from our template. In cases when you need only very simple functionality, you can skip creating a unique controller implementation for your route and just rely on the default implementation that Ember assigns to your route. Now, let's create the addNew action to go in our route.

---

**Avoiding Controllers**

 There's another reason for not choosing to rely heavily on controllers. The Ember team plans to deprecate controllers early in the 2.x release cycle, in favor of performing similar work in the route or in components. Future versions of this book will follow suit, and for now, we're avoiding using controllers as much as possible.

---

Edit the register route so it looks like this:

```
ch1/ember-note/app/register/route.js
import Ember from 'ember';

export default Ember.Route.extend({
  actions: {
    addNew: function() {
      var user = this.store.createRecord('user', {
        name : this.controller.get('name')
      });
      user.save().then(() => {
        console.log('save successful');
        this.controller.set('message','A new user with the name "'
          + this.controller.get('name') + '" was added!');
        this.controller.set('name',null);
      }, function() {
        console.log('save failed');
      });
    }
  }
});
```

The first thing we do here is to add an actions hash to the route. A *hash* is a list of name-value pairs. In this case, the names are names of functions, and the values are the function definitions. We have one function, addNew. This function will be called when we click the button in our user interface, because that's how it was defined in the template.

We're also relying on a bit of new ES 2015 syntax here. The code () =>, known as a *fat arrow function*, will let us continue to use this within the body of the then function, and this will continue to refer to the route object. The call to createRecord uses the Ember Data framework to create a new instance of a model object, and the subsequent call to save saves that record to persistent storage. Ember Data provides access to data over RESTful services. Before we test all of this, we'll need to set up a mock service for Ember Data to call, and a model object to use that data. Let's do that now.

## Adding a Data Service

Ember and Ember CLI offer two ways to provide data to your app during development: fixtures and mock services. While fixtures are easier to set up, mock services offer you the ability to more fully test your code by requiring you to implement everything required to access a RESTful service. So we use mock services in this book. If you're more concerned with testing your core Ember classes, and you're not worried about data access layer testing, you might consider fixtures, which are essentially classes with hardcoded data and simple access methods.

In fact, we go an extra step beyond mock services: our services will persist data across a restart so that as we build the app we'll also see data accumulate. The default mock services created by Ember CLI don't do this, and although this behavior might be preferable for developing an app under normal circumstances, I'd prefer that our data survive a service restart so that our test data is maintained as we work through the examples. So, let's see how a mock service works.

We start by creating a model class for our user object. At the moment, our user consists of one data attribute: the name. Let's use Ember CLI to generate a stub class.

```
$ ember generate model user
```

Here's the class, with implementation details added in:

ch1/ember-note/app/models/user.js
```
import DS from 'ember-data';

export default DS.Model.extend({
  name: DS.attr('string')
});
```

This class relies on the Ember Data libraries to create an instance of a Model, with a single attribute called name. This attribute has a type of string, meaning it will hold text. That's it. This is all we need to model our user object. Now, to interact with the service we're planning to create, we need a RESTAdapter and a RESTSerializer.

To create our RESTAdapter, run the following command:

```
$ ember generate adapter application
```

This creates a RESTAdapter that will be used by the entire application, which is why we named it application. Now, edit the resulting file so it looks like this:

ch1/ember-note/app/adapters/application.js
```
import DS from 'ember-data';

export default DS.RESTAdapter.extend({
  namespace: 'api'
});
```

Similarly, to create the RESTSerializer, run this command:

```
$ ember generate serializer application
```

And the resulting class will look like this:

ch1/ember-note/app/serializers/application.js
```
import DS from 'ember-data';

export default DS.RESTSerializer.extend({});
```

The RESTAdapter has just one purpose: to define the path on the server where we can find our RESTful service. The RESTSerializer is an empty implementation, as we're using default functionality. Because we're going to create a service that exposes the expected API for each model object, this is all we need to do. We'll see a lot more on these in *Adapt to a Nonconventional API*, on page 77 and *Use Serializers to Access Legacy APIs*, on page 82.

Generally, this is where your Ember development would stop. Creating a service to provide data is generally out of the scope of what you'd be doing with Ember, which is a front-end framework, and not for developing REST services. As I said earlier, we're creating a mock service that our app can use for testing and then taking it one step further by making the data persistent.

To make our data persistent, we need to be able to do two things that we can't do just yet. First, we need a place to put the data. For that we'll use the NEDB project, which is an embedded datastore for use with Node. This is a great tool to use for development datastores, such as ours. You'll likely want something more robust for production datastores. Run the following command from within your ember-note directory (the --save-dev flag makes this a dev-only dependency, not a production dependency):

```
$ npm install nedb --save-dev
```

This makes the NEDB project available. When the Ember Data store saves our new user record in the register route, it POSTs data to our mock service over HTTP. So we also need to be able to parse the body of the incoming HTTP request. Get the following library to do this:

```
$ npm install body-parser --save-dev
```

Now we're ready to create our mock service by running the following command:

```
$ ember generate http-mock users
```

With our service created, we just need to add a few lines of code to make use of the libraries we just added, and to respond to a request to create a new record. Take a look at the following code, which makes changes to the basic mock service that let it store data in NEDB:

ch1/ember-note/server/mocks/users.js
```
module.exports = function(app) {
  var express = require('express');
  var usersRouter = express.Router();

  // Use the body-parser library in this service
  var bodyParser = require('body-parser');
  app.use(bodyParser.json());

  // Create an embedded table using NEDB if it doesn't yet exist
  var nedb = require('nedb');
  var userDB = new nedb({ filename : 'users', autoload: true});

  // The POST URL is used to create a new record
  usersRouter.post('/', function(req, res) {

    // Look for the most recently created record and use it to set the id
    // field of our incoming record, which is required by Ember Data
    userDB.find({}).sort({id : -1}).limit(1).exec(function(err,users) {
      if(users.length != 0)
        req.body.user.id = users[0].id + 1;
      else
        req.body.user.id = 1;

      // Insert the new record into our datastore, and return the newly
      // created record to Ember Data
      userDB.insert(req.body.user, function(err,newUser) {
        res.status(201);
        res.send(
          JSON.stringify(
          {
            user : newUser
          }));
      });
    })
  });

  // For now, we won't touch the rest of this code, which was created by
  // Ember CLI
  usersRouter.get('/', function(req, res) {
```

```
      res.send({
        'users': []
      });
    });

    usersRouter.get('/:id', function(req, res) {
      res.send({
        'users': {
          id: req.params.id
        }
      });
    });

    usersRouter.put('/:id', function(req, res) {
    });

    usersRouter.delete('/:id', function(req, res) {
      res.status(204).end();
    });

    app.use('/api/users', usersRouter);
};
```

And with that, we're ready to try out our register feature. If it's not already running, go to a command line and start your app by running the following (if it's already running, you may want to stop it by pressing Ctrl-C, then start it again):

```
$ ember serve
```

Then navigate to localhost:4200, click the register link, provide a username, and click Add. You should see a message that says your user was added, as shown here.

If you want to verify, you can look at the users file in the ember-note directory. You should see something like this:

```
{"name":"newuser1@pragprog.com","id":1,"_id":"8EszAw3RuDxYCIBh"}
```

If that's something like what you're seeing, congratulations! You've completed your first step in learning Ember. Have a drink, take a walk, or just relax how you see fit.

### Ember Addon: Ember CLI Mirage

You can see that we jumped through a few hoops to get a back end working with Ember CLI. Ember CLI's HTTP Mocks are a great way to serve up data using a mock server, but I want to mention one other alternative called Ember CLI Mirage.

Ember CLI Mirage is an Ember addon that accomplishes many of the same goals as Ember CLI's HTTP Mocks, but does so entirely client-side (that is, without requiring you to stand up a Node server to serve mock data). An *Ember addon* is a packaged piece of code that a community member has shared and published to a repository, generally npm, for use by the broader community.

Ember CLI Mirage allows you to create mock data services that run in your browser or in your continuous integration environment. This enables your test classes to test your model layer without requiring an existing back-end server, even a mock one.

Throughout the book I'll mention Ember addons that are worth looking into. Often these will represent an alternative way of performing a task we discussed in the book, or a more mature way of performing a task we performed in a simple way. I make no claims as to whether or not these addons are production-grade. At a minimum, they should be useful for helping you to further explore the Ember ecosystem and to use as a tool for additional learning, as all are open source. We'll cover addons in their own chapter in Chapter 9, *Building and Using Ember Addons*, on page 121.

For the complete documentation on how to use Ember CLI Mirage, take a look at www.ember-cli-mirage.com.

## Next Steps

We covered a large number of ideas in this first chapter. You've seen a small example of each of the major classes in Ember and written a sample application that makes use of a data-aware service. Still, there's a lot more to Ember than what we've covered, and you have a lot left to learn before we're done. Our next step is to begin to build the user interface, first by digging deeper into routes.

# CHAPTER 2

# Directing Traffic with Routes

Now that we've installed Ember and Ember CLI and used them to create an app that lets users register, we're ready to dig into the major features of Ember. The first feature we'll look at is Ember routes. As I mentioned in Chapter 1, the idea of the route is one of the core principles behind Ember. A *route* is the starting point for a single unit of your app's functionality. The hierarchy of routes makes up the organizational structure of your app.

Routes are really, really important in Ember. Fortunately, they are also a really good place to start. In this chapter we'll look at how to use Ember CLI to structure your application using routes. You'll learn how to use the Router class to set up your route hierarchy, and how to use the Route class to define a route. We'll also look at how to move between routes using Ember's navigation helpers. And you'll learn how Ember uses your app URL to indicate not just your location in the app, but the records loaded into the UI. To help you keep Router and Route straight, remember that each app has only one Router, and within that Router you define the structure of your app by defining its routes. A Route class implementation is how you define the behavior of a single route.

To learn more about routes, we'll begin to piece together more of EmberNote's feature set by building the app's navigational structure. By the end of this chapter you'll have completed the majority of the route structure of EmberNote, and you'll know how to write the code to navigate between routes.

## Use the Router Class to Organize Your App

In the previous chapter we created the register route for EmberNote. As you can imagine, Ember applications are made up of many routes, each one unique within the application. Taken together, the routes form a hierarchy of distinct locations in the application, exposing each of the features unique to that place in the hierarchy. Ember keeps a record of this hierarchy in a single class, the Router class, as shown in the following figure.

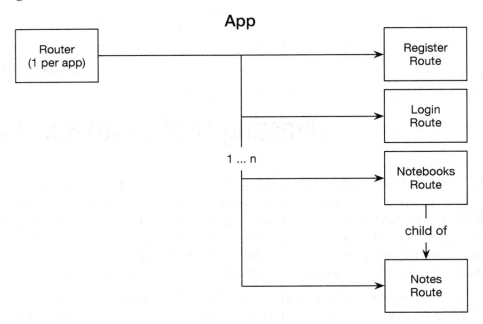

Because we're using Ember CLI to manage our app, we won't directly edit EmberNote's Router all that often. Most of the time we'll allow Ember CLI to do the editing for us.

Let's look at one such example. When we last worked on EmberNote, this is what our Router class looked like:

```
ch2/ember-note/app/router.js
import Ember from 'ember';
import config from './config/environment';

var Router = Ember.Router.extend({
  location: config.locationType
});

Router.map(function() {
  this.route('register');
});

export default Router;
```

Let's add a couple of routes to our app to see what happens to the Router. When users open the EmberNote app, they can register, or if they are already registered, they can log in. Once they log in, they'll see a list of their notebooks.

Let's add two routes now, to let users log in and to let them view their note-books. From within your ember-note directory, run the following commands:

```
$ ember generate route login --pod
$ ember generate route notebooks --pod
```

Having run these commands, you should see two new lines in your router:

```
this.route('login');
this.route('notebooks');
```

The great thing is, Ember CLI will add in new routes as you create them, without wiping out existing changes to your router.

The Router now contains the two new routes we generated via Ember CLI. We'll now be able to define both the login and notebooks routes by building their classes.

We'll create more routes throughout the book, and we'll often check back in on the Router class. It's a good class to come back to periodically, to help us stay anchored and keep the overall app structure in mind. Right now, let's take a look at how to define a route by working through the login route.

## Define Your Routes

As noted previously, each route corresponds to a given URL in your app. We defined four routes in our application with the following URLs:

- http://localhost:4200
- http://localhost;4200/register
- http://localhost:4200/login
- http://localhost:4200/notebooks

We defined register in the first chapter, and we generated the classes for login and notebook just now. The names and paths of these routes correspond to the definitions in router.js.

You may be wondering when we defined the root URL. The answer is that we defined it when we created the application. This route, known as the application route, uses Ember's default implementation of the Route class. We modified a file called application.hbs in the first chapter. This file contains the template for the application route. By simply creating our project with Ember CLI and through Ember's reliance on default functionality, we defined the application route.

This also raises one point about the default Ember structure. Each individual route corresponds to exactly one template. For the application route, this is the application.hbs template. For each of our generated routes, it's the template.hbs template as defined in the route's folder, assuming you've used the --pod flag; otherwise the template is named for the route, and lives in the templates folder.

Let's create the login route now. This route needs to let the user sign into the EmberNote application. It should be available from a link on the main page, just like register was, and let previously registered users sign in with their usernames. Once they've signed in, they should be taken to their list of notebooks (the other route we've generated so far). Further, once they've signed in, the register and login links should no longer appear.

To do this, we're going to make changes to the following files:

- app/template/application.hbs: To add navigation to let the user load the login route, and to hide navigation to register and login once the user has logged in

- app/login/route.js: To define the login action

- app/login/template.hbs: To define the user interface for the login route

To reach the login route, we need to first make it available via the application.hbs file. Edit this file so it looks like the following:

```
ch2/ember-note/app/templates/application.hbs
<div class="container">
  <div class="row">
    <div class="col-md-2">
      Welcome to EmberNote
    </div>
    <div class="col-md-10">
      {{#if user}}
        Hello, {{user.name}}
      {{/if}}
      {{#unless user}}
        {{#link-to 'register'}}register{{/link-to}} 
        {{#link-to 'login'}}login{{/link-to}}
      {{/unless}}
    </div>
  </div>
  <div class="row">
    <div>
      {{outlet}}
    </div>
  </div>
</div>
```

The first addition you'll make to the file is an {{#if}} expression. The text contained within this expression is only displayed if the expression evaluates to true. In this case, if the application controller has a value in the user attribute, the user's name is displayed. We'll see how this user attribute is set when we look at the login route next.

The next section, inside the {{#unless}} expression, is displayed if the user attribute is missing. It contains the {{#link-to}} navigation item for the register route, and our new login route as well.

When users click the link to the login route, they're taken to localhost:4200/login. The login template is rendered into the {{outlet}}, meaning that the content of that template is displayed in the placeholder defined by the {{outlet}} expression. The login template, defined in app/login/template.hbs, looks like this:

ch2/ember-note/app/login/template.hbs
```
<div class="col-md-12">
  Login: {{input value=name}} <button {{action 'login'}}>Login</button>
</div>
```

This template, which is the single template associated to the login route, has a mere two elements. The {{input}} expression results in an HTML text input field being displayed and takes its value from the name attribute. The {{action}} expression results in the login action being executed in the Route, which we define next.

All of this ties together in the login route class, like this:

ch2/ember-note/app/login/route.js
```
import Ember from 'ember';

export default Ember.Route.extend({
  actions: {
    login: function() {
      this.store.query('user', {
        name: this.controller.get('name')
      }).then((users) => {
        if(users.get('length') === 1) {
          var user = users.objectAt(0);
          this.controllerFor('application').set('user',user);
          this.transitionTo('notebooks');
        }
        else {
          console.log('unexpected query result');
        }
      });
    }
  }
});
```

As we saw in Chapter 1, this Route class uses the ES6 module syntax. The first line of the class imports the Ember framework, which is then used when we extend the base Route class in our class declaration. We're using an anonymous declaration and export of the Route. Ember CLI takes the path to the file and uses it to conclude that this class, though declared anonymously, represents the login route.

The next block of code defines the actions hash, which is a name-value pair listing of action names and implementations. Our login route requires only one action, the aptly named login action.

As described earlier in this chapter, the login action verifies that the requested user has properly registered, and then displays the list of the user's notebooks. The next block,

```
this.store.query('user', {
  name : this.controller.get('name')
})
```

executes a query against our server API using the value of the name field from template.hbs as a query parameter. We'll update the API next.

For your login route to work, you need to make a small change to the mock server we created. Open your server/mocks/users.js file and update the get endpoint as follows:

ch2/ember-note/server/mocks/users.js
```
usersRouter.get('/', function(req, res) {
  userDB.find(req.query).exec(function(error,users) {
    res.send({
      'users': users
    });
  });
});
```

Ember CLI should have deployed your changes as you made them, but if for some reason it hasn't, you may need to run the ember serve command from your ember-note directory to catch up. Once you have, visit the login route and try logging into EmberNote. You should be redirected to the notebooks route.

Because the store.find call to the API is asynchronous, it returns a Promise object to the login route. A *Promise* can be described as an object that will eventually resolve to a value. Depending on whether the function is successful or fails, different logic can be executed. Once this Promise has resolved successfully, the function in the then block is executed. First, we check that we received only one row back from the API. Assuming we have, we load the first and only row into the user object. Then, in order to make the {{#if}} and {{#unless}} blocks work properly, we set the user attribute in the application controller. Our last step is to run one of Ember's navigation functions, transitionTo. This function redirects the user to the notebooks route.

### RSVP: Ember's Promise Library

Promises are a widely used idea, without a canonical implementation. ECMAScript 2015 is expected to include a Promise implementation, but in the meantime, Ember relies on RSVP. RSVP is compliant with the in-process specification of ES 2015, but it's available now. It's maintained by members of the core Ember team and available on GitHub at github.com/tildeio/rsvp.js.

We've covered more than just routes in this section to let us build a good example. The key elements for you to focus on now are the {{#link-to}} expression, the transitionTo function, and the actions hash. As used in the application.hbs template, the {{#link-to}} expression allows the user to load the login route's template.hbs into the {{outlet}} in application.hbs, when the resulting link is clicked. For this to work, we need the login route defined in router.js. The {{link-to}} expression is one way of causing the parent route to load a child route into its outlet.

Another way to implement navigation is by using functions like transitionTo to move between routes. As used in the login route, it takes the currently loaded route (as determined by the instance calling the function), and replaces it with the route named in the function call. As noted in our example, we can use this function to indicate not only which route to load, but also which record it should load. We'll see more on how the destination route knows which record to load when we look at setting a route's model shortly.

Last, the actions hash is used to define name-value pairs of actions and their related functions. This concept isn't route-specific, and we'll see more examples of this later, but it's worth noting that one option for action handling is to add your actions to a route in this way.

Now we understand more of what a route is and how it's used, let's take a look at how to use a route to load and display data via the route's model hook.

## Set Your Model

When we're working with a route, the model hook is used to load and supply the necessary data. As we've seen, not every route will implement its model hook, but most will. The model hook is a function, defined within an instance of a Route class, that loads the data to be displayed by that route.

In the EmberNote app, we haven't yet built a route that makes use of the model hook. Let's do so now. When a user signs in via the login action, we use the transitionTo function to transition to the notebooks route. Let's define that route now, and along the way we'll see how to use the model hook.

The notebooks route has a simple purpose: to display a list of the notebooks a user has created in EmberNote. A notebook is a collection of notes, so clicking on a notebook in the notebooks route will then display a list of that notebook's notes. Here's the notebooks route:

```
ch2/ember-note/app/notebooks/route.js
import Ember from 'ember';

export default Ember.Route.extend({
  model: function(params) {
    return this.store.query('notebook',{user: params.user_id});
  },
  actions: {
  }
});
```

Similar to the login route, notebooks uses the ES6 module format and begins with the necessary import statement. Further, we defined it using the --pod command-line flag, so the file is called route.js and resides in the app/notebooks path, and the definition uses the export default Ember.Route.extend form.

The model hook is the first block in the body of our Route. It's defined as a function, which is executed by Ember when the route is loaded. You'll also note that an object, known as params, is passed to this function. We'll come back to this shortly.

The body of the model hook contains some Ember Data code to load the logged-in user's notebooks. We'll cover Ember Data further in Chapter 5, *Modeling Your Data*, on page 63, so let's focus on the route-specific portions of the code now. This line of code causes Ember Data to query for notebook objects that are owned by the user with params.user_id. So where does this user_id come from?

To provide the params object to the route, and specifically the user_id, we need to use a path segment in our route definition. Let's look at the definition of the notebooks route in the router.js file:

```
ch2/ember-note/app/router.js
this.route('notebooks', { path:'notebooks/:user_id'}, function() {});
```

This is how you use the Router class to define a route with a path segment. In Ember, a path segment is used to provide a value that can be used to load a record in the route. For this route, we're using the id of the logged-on user to identify the notebooks we want to load. Defining your route this way in the Router class, and then using the params object in the Route, allows you to provide the data necessary to load the notebooks. Of course, the object that initiated the navigation to this route needs to add that data to the path in the first place. In our case, we need to modify the transitionTo function in the login route to provide this data:

ch2/ember-note/app/login/route.js
```
this.transitionTo('notebooks', user.get('id'));
```

With the correct data, we're able to initiate a query against our API to get the current user's notebook data.

---

**Security Note**

Using path segments to pass data between routes is an extremely useful feature of Ember, but it's easy to use in a way that can be insecure. Placing cleartext data in your URL is a potential risk, given that it's easy for a malicious user to change in an attempt to break your application's security. This is known as a direct object reference vulnerability, and you can read more about it at www.owasp.org/index.php/Top_10_2010-A4-Insecure_Direct_Object_References.

---

Next, we need to define the notebook API. To do this, run the following command to create the mock service and provide a REST service to our route:

```
$ ember generate http-mock notebooks
```

We then populate the resulting file with the following code (I won't go through the full explanation of what's happening; it's in essence the same code as we used for the users service in *Adding a Data Service*, on page 12):

ch2/ember-note/server/mocks/notebooks.js
```
module.exports = function(app) {
  var express = require('express');
  var notebooksRouter = express.Router();
  var bodyParser = require('body-parser');
  app.use(bodyParser.json());
  var nedb = require('nedb');
  var notebookDB = new nedb({ filename : 'notebooks', autoload: true});

  notebooksRouter.get('/', function(req, res) {
    notebookDB.find(req.query).exec(function(error,notebooks) {
      res.send({
        'notebooks': notebooks
      });
    });
  });
});
```

```
notebooksRouter.post('/', function(req, res) {
  notebookDB.find({}).sort({id : -1}).limit(1).exec(
    function(err,notebooks) {
      if(notebooks.length != 0)
        req.body.notebook.id =  notebooks[0].id + 1;
      else
        req.body.notebook.id = 1;
      notebookDB.insert(req.body.notebook,function(err,newNotebook) {
        res.status(201);
        res.send(
          JSON.stringify(
          {
            notebook : newNotebook
          }));
      });
    })
});

notebooksRouter.get('/:id', function(req, res) {
  res.send({
    'notebooks': {
      id: req.params.id
    }
  });
});

notebooksRouter.put('/:id', function(req, res) {
  res.send({
    'notebooks': {
      id: req.params.id
    }
  });
});

notebooksRouter.delete('/:id', function(req, res) {
  res.status(204).end();
});

app.use('/api/notebooks', notebooksRouter);
};
```

We also need to define the model class. Run this command to define a model class for the notebook type:

```
$ ember generate model notebook
```

There's much more to come on models later. Right now, add the following code to your notebook.js file:

ch2/ember-note/app/models/notebook.js
```
import DS from 'ember-data';

export default DS.Model.extend({
  title: DS.attr('string'),
  user: DS.belongsTo('user'),
  notes: DS.hasMany('note')
});
```

We'll also go ahead and define the mock service and model for the note object, which notebook relies on. Run the following command:

```
$ ember generate http-mock notes
```

And update the resulting service with this code:

ch2/ember-note/server/mocks/notes.js
```
module.exports = function(app) {
  var express = require('express');
  var notesRouter = express.Router();
  var bodyParser = require('body-parser');
  app.use(bodyParser.json());
  var nedb = require('nedb');
  var noteDB = new nedb({ filename : 'notes', autoload: true});

  notesRouter.get('/', function(req, res) {
    noteDB.find(req.query).exec(function(error,notes) {
      res.send({
        'notes': notes
      });
    });
  });

  notesRouter.post('/', function(req, res) {
    noteDB.find({}).sort({id : -1}).limit(1).exec(function(err,notes) {
      if(notes.length != 0)
        req.body.note.id =  notes[0].id + 1;
      else
        req.body.note.id = 1;
      noteDB.insert(req.body.note,function(err,newNote) {
        res.status(201);
        res.send(
          JSON.stringify(
          {
            note : newNote
          }));
      });
    })
  });
```

```
notesRouter.get('/:id', function(req, res) {
  res.send({
    'notes': {
      id: req.params.id
    }
  });
});

notesRouter.put('/:id', function(req, res) {
  var id = parseInt(req.params.id);
  noteDB.update({id: id}, {$set: req.body.note},
    function(err, numReplaced, newNotes) {
      res.send({
        'notes': {
          id: id
        }
      });
    }
  );
});

notesRouter.delete('/:id', function(req, res) {
  var id = parseInt(req.params.id);
  noteDB.remove({id: id}, function(err,numRemoved) {
    res.status(204).end();
  });
});

app.use('/api/notes', notesRouter);
};
```

Now run this command to create the model:

```
$ ember generate model note
```

And define the model as follows:

ch2/ember-note/app/models/note.js
```
import DS from 'ember-data';

export default DS.Model.extend({
  title: DS.attr('string'),
  body: DS.attr('string'),
  notebook: DS.belongsTo('notebook')
});
```

Don't worry if you have questions about the model classes now. We'll discuss these in Chapter 5, *Modeling Your Data*, on page 63. With the notebooks web service set up we're ready to create the template for the notebooks route. As you've learned, the template is used to render the user interface for a route.

In this case we want to create an interface that allows users to do two things: (1) create a new notebook, and (2) display the list of existing notebooks. Here's the template that you'll want to create:

```
ch2/ember-note/app/notebooks/template.hbs
<div>
  <div class="col-md-3">
    <div>Notebooks</div>
    <div>
      title: {{input value=title}}
      <button {{action 'addNotebook'}}>Add</button>
    </div>
    <div>
      <ul>
        {{#each model as |notebook|}}
          {{#link-to 'notebooks.notes' notebook.id}}
            <li>{{notebook.title}}</li>
          {{/link-to}}
        {{else}}
          <div>No notebooks found</div>
        {{/each}}
      </ul>
    </div>
  </div>
  <div class="col-md-9">
    {{outlet}}
  </div>
</div>
```

I won't dwell too much on the template code now—we'll go into more detail in the next chapter. What I'd like you to notice is that we're directly referencing the model from our template. As I mentioned earlier in this chapter, in the absence of directly creating a controller class, we can rely on default functionality of the base Ember.Controller class. This class has a model variable, and by default it calls the route's model hook to populate this variable.

For the notebooks route, the Ember Data query returns zero or more rows. In the template.hbs file, the model referenced is the variable contained the default controller. To get at the data in the variable, we're using an {{#each}} expression, which loops along a list of model instances. The model variable in a controller can contain either a single model instance or an array of model instances.

Our template displays the notebooks titles in an unordered list. We'll dig into the details of the template and expressions later. For now, your list is probably empty. Let's see how to use actions to add to the list and reload your template so they're displayed. Add this code to the actions hash in your notebooks route:

```
ch2/ember-note/app/notebooks/route.js
addNotebook: function() {
  var notebook = this.store.createRecord('notebook', {
    title: this.controller.get('title'),
    user: this.controllerFor('application').get('user')
  });
  notebook.save().then(() => {
    console.log('save successful');
    this.controller.set('title',null);
    this.refresh();
  }, function() {
    console.log('save failed');
  });
}
```

This action uses Ember Data to create a new record. It populates the record with values from our template and populates the user field of our notebook model by loading the data from the application controller: user: this.controllerFor('application').get('user').

Once the record has been saved with Ember Data, we clear out the UI fields and then refresh the list using this.refresh(). This reloads the model from the server and displays your new record.

We've focused in this section on the parts of a Route implementation that relate to displaying data. We've had to touch on a few other concepts as well, such as templates and models, which we'll cover in more detail later in the book. Don't worry if you don't fully understand these right now. There's a lot more to discuss. What I hope you understand is how to use path segments, the model hook, and the related navigation functions like transitionTo to work with data. The rest of this chapter will focus largely on navigation between routes, and on creating a hierarchy of routes in your application. We'll start there by adding the first route that will be a child to the routes we've created: the note route.

## Nest Routes

So far we've only added routes that sit one level below the application route. Let's get a bit further into the weeds and add a child route of a child route, also known as a *nested* route. Run this command:

```
$ ember generate route notebooks/notes --pod
```

This route will be used to display all notes that are part of a given notebook. As you might expect, the previous command created a new entry in the Router. I've added the following path segment information to app/router.js:

```
this.route("notebooks", { path:"notebooks/:user_id"}, function() {
  this.route("notes", { path:"notes/:notebook_id"}, function() {});
});
```

Define the route class by updating it to look like the following (we'll need this later).

ch2/ember-note/app/notebooks/notes/route.js

```
import Ember from 'ember';

export default Ember.Route.extend({
  model: function(params) {
    return this.store.query('note', {notebook:params.notebook_id});
  },
  actions: {
    addNote: function() {
      this.store.findRecord('notebook',
        this.paramsFor('notebooks.notes').notebook_id).then(
          (notebook) => {
            console.log(notebook);
            var note = this.store.createRecord('note', {
              title : this.controller.get('title'),
              notebook: notebook
            });
            console.log(note);
            note.save().then(() => {
              console.log('save successful');
              this.controller.set('title',null);
              this.refresh();
            }, function() {
              console.log('save failed');
            });
          });
    },
    deleteNote: function(note) {
      console.log('deleting note with title ' + note.get('title'));
      note.deleteRecord();
      note.save();
    }
  }
});
```

And your new notes template should look like this:

ch2/ember-note/app/notebooks/notes/template.hbs

```
<div class="col-md-12">
  Notes
</div>
<div>
  <div class="col-md-4">
    <div>
```

```
      title: {{input value=title}} <button {{action 'addNote'}}>Add</button>
  </div>
  <div>
    <ul>
      {{#each model as |note|}}
        <li>
          {{#link-to 'notebooks.notes.note' note.id}}
            {{note.title}}
          {{/link-to}}
          <button {{action 'deleteNote' note}}>delete</button>
        </li>
      {{/each}}
    </ul>
  </div>
</div>
<div class="col-md-8">
  {{outlet}}
</div>
</div>
```

This is known as a nested route, so called because it resides, and only has meaning, as a child of the notebooks route. The command also created the route's files, route.js and template.hbs, under notebooks/notes, a new directory. We filled out the implementations earlier.

---

**The Missing Note Route**

If you look closely at the new notes template, you'll notice we added a link to a child route that doesn't yet exist. This is why you don't see newly added notes if you add them. Ember isn't able to render the link because the child route is missing, and there's likely an error in your browser console. Don't worry! We'll get to defining the note route in Chapter 4, *Building In Reuse with Components*, on page 49.

---

You can navigate to this route and define it, just as you would the notebooks route, except that your {{#link-to}} expression resides in the notebooks template. We'll spend more time with the notes route and adding a child route to it in Chapter 4, when we build a feature to edit notes. Let's look at a few more options for navigation before we wrap up our exploration of routes.

## Transition Between Routes

Many times you will want to move from one section of your app to another in response to an action. Ember provides you with a few options to do this. One such option is the transitionTo function. We've used this previously to transition from the login route to the notebooks route:

```
ch2/ember-note/app/login/route.js
this.transitionTo('notebooks', user.get('id'));
```

The first argument to this function is the name of the route you're transitioning to. You can provide either a top-level route, such as notebooks, or a nested route, such as notebooks.notes. You can provide other information as well, such as a specific model, in the second argument to the function. If you provide a model, the receiving route will use that model when rendering. If you provide a literal, as we've done here, the receiving route will call its model hook, and use that literal as a parameter to load the model.

This is one simple way to move from one route to another. It's important to note that the target route will be rendered into the same {{outlet}} as the calling route is currently rendered into. If you want to really get fancy, the render function is for you, and we'll look at that next.

## Render Templates into Named Outlets

In addition to the transtionTo function, Ember provides a function with more fine-grained control over transitions: the render function. Using the render function, you can not only control which route you're rendering, but also where you're rendering it and what data and controller to use.

So far, we've only used the default {{outlet}} expressions to contain our templates. Ember also allows you to create named outlets, simply by providing a name to the outlet: {{outlet 'namedOutlet'}}.

If you want to use the render function, you'll need to name the affected outlets. The render function accepts a name, which represents the name of the template you want to render, and an options object. The options object can have any of the following parameters:

into
: This is the name of the template you want to render your template into. If you leave this parameter out, Ember will use the parent template of the template that you named earlier.

outlet
: This is the name of the outlet on the template named in the into parameter. If this parameter is left out, Ember uses the default outlet.

controller
: The controller class to use in rendering the new template. If not defined, Ember will use the default.

model
: An instance of the model class to use in rendering the new template. Ember will run the target route's model hook if not specified.

The render function is useful for cases when you might want to change the template displayed in an outlet that resides somewhere outside of the current route's hierarchy. Being able to specifically name the template and location allows you a high level of navigational control, even in areas that the current route might not always need to be concerned with.

## Next Steps

As noted at the beginning of the chapter, the route pattern is a key feature in Ember. It offers you a way to clearly reason about how your application is assembled, and help you understand how to move from one app feature to another. We've seen a few of the features that you get by using Ember routes. There are many more, but we have plenty of other ground to cover first. Our next stop is a close sibling of the route. As you've learned, each route corresponds to exactly one template, which is used by Ember to render the user interface for a given route. In the next chapter, we'll look at the template feature and the Handlebars and HTMLBars expression languages.

# CHAPTER 3

# Laying Out a User Interface

With a solid understanding of how to organize your application using routes, let's talk about their sibling: the template. In Ember, as you might expect, a *template* contains a chunk of your user interface code. It consists of HTML, CSS, and Handlebars expressions.

In this chapter, you'll learn how Ember's architecture supports the use of templates. You'll also learn more about how to create templates, relate them to one another via the route structure, and use the Handlebars expression language to work with Ember objects. In addition, you'll learn how to use a variety of expressions already in the Ember framework to add controls and display logic to your user interface.

Let's jump into the first template you'll create for each app you create: the aptly named application template.

## Make Your App with a Single Page

The sort of application you'll create using Ember is known as a *single-page application*, because the application is written in such a way that all of your content is rendered via one HTML page, and changes to that page are done via DOM manipulation and Ajax.

In Ember, when using Ember CLI, that page is known as index.html. We looked at it in Chapter 1, but let's look again at our index.html for EmberNote:

ch3/ember-note/app/index.html

```
<!DOCTYPE html>
<html>
  <head>
    <meta charset="utf-8">
    <meta http-equiv="X-UA-Compatible" content="IE=edge">
    <title>EmberNote</title>
    <meta name="description" content="">
```

```
<meta name="viewport" content="width=device-width, initial-scale=1">

{{content-for 'head'}}

<link rel="stylesheet" href="assets/vendor.css">
<link rel="stylesheet" href="assets/ember-note.css">

{{content-for 'head-footer'}}
</head>
<body>
{{content-for 'body'}}

<script src="assets/vendor.js"></script>
<script src="assets/ember-note.js"></script>

{{content-for 'body-footer'}}
</body>
</html>
```

This file was built by Ember CLI, and with the exception of our change to the title, it's exactly what Ember CLI generated when we created our new app. You might notice that there's no reference to any template in this file. The {{content-for}} hooks are there for Ember CLI addons, but we're not using those. So how does our app even begin to be rendered?

The key lies in the ember-note.js file. This file is generated by the Ember CLI build process and includes every line of code you've written so far, and many more that you haven't. If you're curious, you can take a look at this file. What you need to know is that in order to render your user interface, this file has the logic to create your DOM structure on the fly based on the templates you create and all of the other supporting classes. It then inserts this structure into the page, and your user interface is presented to the user.

The first template that sits at the root of your template hierarchy is the application template. It resides in application.hbs, shown here:

ch3/ember-note/app/templates/application.hbs
```
<div class="container">
  <div class="row">
    <div class="col-md-2">
      Welcome to EmberNote
    </div>
    <div class="col-md-10">
      {{#if user}}
        Hello, {{user.name}}
      {{/if}}
      {{#unless user}}
        {{#link-to 'register'}}register{{/link-to}} 
        {{#link-to 'login'}}login{{/link-to}}
```

```
        {{/unless}}
      </div>
    </div>
    <div class="row">
      <div>
        {{outlet}}
      </div>
    </div>
</div>
```

We've spent a fair amount of time in this file in Chapter 1, but let's take a look at the templating features. The file is a mix of HTML and an expression language, which is known as *Handlebars*. We'll get into the various expressions you see in this template throughout this chapter. What's special about this template is that it sits at the root of your template hierarchy. Therefore, it is the jumping-off point of the entire app. In our case, any child template we decide to render will be rendered into the main {{outlet}} receptacle.

---

**Handlebars**

Handlebars is a part of Ember that you'll use quite often, even though it's so deeply integrated you may not realize it. Ember uses the HTMLBars variant of Handlebars, which is made available to your app via an addon called ember-cli-htmlbars.

Whenever you use one of the components we'll discuss in this chapter, you're relying on Handlebars. Handlebars is two things, really. First, it's a templating framework written in JavaScript and based on Mustache. Second, it's an expression language, as codified in the templating framework. You'll learn most of what you need to know about Handlebars just by using it, but if you're the curious sort, you can learn more by visiting handlebarsjs.com and github.com/tildeio/htmlbars.

---

As we saw in Chapter 2, the EmberNote route hierarchy has three routes one level below the application route: register, login, and notebooks. Any one of these routes can be rendered into the {{outlet}}. There's nothing to prevent you from trying to render a route that's deeper in the hierarchy, but without the expected backing data loaded into your route's model, it will probably not work correctly.

Our layout is fairly simple, so there are some options we're not using. If you think about a more sophisticated example, you're likely to have multiple outlets available on the application template. For example, you may have an outlet for the left menu, an outlet for the top menu, an outlet for the main section of the page, and so on. In this case you would use named outlets, and use techniques from *Render Templates into Named Outlets*, on page 33 to render routes into those outlets.

Let's take a closer look now at how to create and define a template, and then we'll see some of the controls you can add using Handlebars.

# Segment Your UI into Templates

Each user interface is composed of distinct groupings of controls, such as a menu, a table, or a form, that can be naturally separated into templates (or components, which we'll see next). A good design step when working with Ember is to take a look at your planned user interface and draw boundaries around associated sets of controls. Once you've defined the control groups that can be represented by one data model, you have a template! Let's take a look at how exactly you create one.

## Creating a Template

When you create a route with Ember CLI, a template is created for you to use within that route. If you're using the --pod flag, the template for your new route is in the route's directory and is named template.hbs. Otherwise, it's in the templates directory and is called myroute.hbs, where "myroute" is the name of the route you defined. The decision of when to use the --pod flag is primarily an organizational one, and you should decide based on what makes sense to you. I prefer to keep related templates and routes in the same directory, so I choose to use the --pod flag.

When Ember CLI creates a new template in this way, the only thing it adds to the template is an {{outlet}} expression for your child routes. It's up to you to add the rest! Let's look at another, more interesting template, the notebooks template:

```
ch3/ember-note/app/notebooks/template.hbs
<div>
  <div class="col-md-3">
    <div>Notebooks</div>
    <div>
      title: {{input value=title}}
      <button {{action 'addNotebook'}}>Add</button>
    </div>
    <div>
      <ul>
        {{#each model as |notebook|}}
          {{#link-to 'notebooks.notes' notebook.id}}
            <li>{{notebook.title}}</li>
```

```
        {{/link-to}}
      {{else}}
        <div>No notebooks found</div>
      {{/each}}
    </ul>
  </div>
</div>
<div class="col-md-9">
  {{outlet}}
</div>
</div>
```

Within the template, you see a mix of HTML and Handlebars expressions (which are anything within a double set of curly braces). This particular snippet includes a few HTML tags for structure, but most interesting are the Handlebars expressions. Let's take a look at a very important one now.

## Linking Templates Together

One Handlebars expression in this template is the {{#each}} expression. This represents a basic looping construct. Recall that each template is bound to one and only one route and controller. One purpose of a route is to provide data to its associated template. Here the route provides a list of zero to many notebook objects to the notebooks template. The {{#each}} expression is evaluated for each notebook object. If the route provides an empty list, the {{else}} segment of the expression will be evaluated, and the page will display "No notebooks found" to the user.

The following code is then evaluated for each of the notebook objects within the list:

```
<div>
  {{#link-to 'notebooks.notes' notebook.id}}
  {{notebook.title}}{{/link-to}}
</div>
```

This is a {{link-to}} expression. At runtime, this {{#link-to}} snippet evaluates to roughly the following HTML:

```
<a id="ember100" class="ember-view" href="notebooks/10/notes/1">Notebook</a>
```

Let's break down this link. The {{#link-to}} expression generates a route, including each of the necessary path segments. In this case, we are already on the notebooks route, having loaded it for a user with an id value of "10." We're trying to navigate from there to the notes child route, with a notebook with an id of "1."

While this HTML is interesting, it's how Ember uses this link that matters most. When you click the link, Ember updates the current URL to http://local-host:4200/notebooks/1/notes/1 (the numbers may vary slightly, but the other segments should be the same). Ember renders the notebooks template into the {{outlet}} in the application template, and the notes template into the {{outlet}} on the notebooks template. You can then add child routes to the notes route, and so forth.

The following figure illustrates the relationship between URL segments and nested templates.

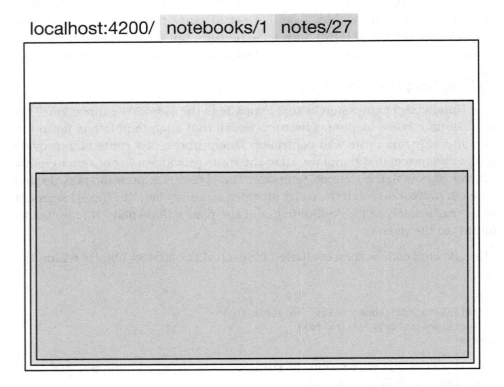

The relationship between URLs and the exact location in the app, including the data loaded, is one of the killer features of Ember. When used this way, the URL becomes a complete representation of both the user's current location (where in the app the user is) and the currently loaded data (which record is visible). The resulting URL will consistently display the same information when loaded, which enables easy sharing.

When working with a real-world app, your goal is to present information to your users in a way that makes sense. That information will almost always have relationships between pieces of data, and those relationships result in a hierarchy. To display hierarchical data your user interface will have hierarchies of screens or widgets. In Ember, those screens or widgets are encapsulated by a template. So while a template is very nearly a stand-alone piece of functionality, you'll also need to consider each template in relation to those near it.

The ability to arrange templates in a hierarchy and use the URL to capture the state of the app are two of Ember's most helpful features. But there's a lot more about templates that is useful for developers. Next up, let's take a look at how to use Handlebars expressions to render some standard HTML controls.

# Render HTML Controls with Expressions

So far we've used some pretty vanilla controls to illustrate Ember's templating system. But the Handlebars expression language and Ember's helper classes are capable of rendering a great deal more variety than that.

In this section we'll go through the most useful controls available in Ember. We'll start with how to use Ember to display static data, and then talk about conditionals and looping. Then we'll visit input controls and wrap up by going over actions and links.

## Rendering Data

The most fundamental use of Handlebars expressions is to simply display data from the route and its related controller. A *controller* is a class used to provide access to the data supplied via the route's model hook. Recall that each template is bound to one and only one route. This is also true for controllers. Each controller maintains a set of properties, which are data that can be used by the template. Thus far, we haven't needed to explicitly define a controller class and have relied on default functionality in the framework. However, if we want to display the data for a given controller property, we simply add it to an expression in our template, like this:

```
<div>{{propertyName}}</div>
```

Whatever data is held in that property will be displayed as static text on the page. If your controller looks like this:

```
import Ember from 'ember'

export default Ember.Controller.extend({
  propertyName: "A value"
});
```

then the previous expression will render this:

```
<div>A value</div>
```

It's possible for a controller to manage the data of just one record, which is called an ObjectController, or many records, which is called an ArrayController. In our example, the controller that backs the notebooks template is an ArrayController. If you have an ArrayController, you can render data from the list of records it manages by using the {{each}} expression, as we saw earlier in the chapter. Let's now turn to Ember's control flow expressions.

## Controlling Templates with Looping and Conditionals

Ember has a number of different means of controlling what is displayed within a template. One such construct is the {{if}} expression. An {{if}} expression renders a section of the template (or not) based on whether the provided property is true, or whether it's false, null, undefined, or []. (Oh, JavaScript.)

To use an {{if}} expression, you'll surround the block you want to conditionally include, like this:

```
{{#if condition}}
  <div>HELLO</div>
{{else}}
  <div>never mind</div>
{{/if}}
```

Ember refers to such an expression as a *block expression,* because a block of template code is surrounded by the expression. Block expressions require an opening and closing tag (for example, {{#if}} and {{/if}}). In this case, "HELLO" will be rendered if condition is true; otherwise "never mind" will be rendered.

Ember also allows you to chain together conditions, rather than nest them within your {{else}} block. If you have two, three, or forty-seven conditions that you need to chain together, you can do so like this:

```
{{#if condition}}
  <div>HELLO</div>
{{else if condition2}}
  <div>never mind</div>
{{else if condition3}}
  <div>WAT</div>
{{else}}
  <div>go away</div>
{{/if}}
```

You can also shortcut the standard {{if}} syntax by using an inline if:

```
{{if condition 'on' 'off'}}
```

The second and third parameters to the inline conditional can contain a property or a string, but nothing more. The {{if}} expression has a sibling expression called {{unless}}. Use this expression when you have one outcome in which to render the body of the expression, and you don't want to confuse matters by "not"-ing the conditional, like this:

```
{{#unless hasChrome}}
  The Chrome web browser is required to run this app.
{{/unless}}
```

The admonishment to use only Chrome is displayed unless the user has the Chrome browser. The hasChrome variable is a value provided by the backing model or route attributes, and isn't a standard part of Ember. Yes, you could also use an {{if}}, but this combination of expression and property reads a bit more clearly. You'll notice we used these expressions in our application.hbs template.

You've already seen the code to loop over a list of items using {{each}} earlier in this chapter, so I won't repeat it. I will remind you that {{each}} requires that your controller reference a list of records as its model.

## Binding Input Fields

Every expression we've seen thus far is geared toward displaying static text. A lot of Ember's power comes from its ability to link editable fields to the controller, so we need to use input fields as well. Let's update our example to use input fields now.

Start by taking a look at the notebooks template:

```
ch3/ember-note/app/notebooks/template.hbs
title: {{input value=title}}
<button {{action 'addNotebook'}}>Add</button>
```

A minimal {{input}} expression such as this renders the following HTML:

```
<input type="text" value="Notebook Title" />
```

We didn't explicitly define a type for the input field, but Ember set it to "text" by default. The other option is to set it explicitly, like this:

```
{{input type="text" value=title}}
```

This renders the equivalent HTML. If you look closely you'll see that the type attribute is set to a quoted string, while value is set to an unquoted string.

This distinction is important. A quoted string will be rendered in the HTML exactly as written; an unquoted string will render the value of the given controller property.

The following HTML attributes can also be set for an input field:

| | | | | |
|---|---|---|---|---|
| accept | autocomplete | autofocus | autosave | disabled |
| form | formaction | formenctype | formmethod | formnovalidate |
| formtarget | height | inputmode | max | maxlength |
| min | multiple | name | pattern | placeholder |
| readonly | required | selectionDirection | size | spellcheck |
| step | tabindex | value | width | |

In addition to HTML attributes, the {{input}} expression supports event handlers, or *actions*, as they are known in Ember. You can link to an action from your {{input}} expression like so:

```
{{input type="text" value=name action="execute"}}
```

In the previous example, the value attribute is bound to a variable in the backing controller. The value may be bound or unbound. If it's bound, it won't need quotes; if it's unbound, you provide the exact string you want to set into the value of the field, within quotes.

The action property is bound to the Return key press event. When Return is pressed, the named action is called. A number of other user events may be bound by setting the name of the event to an action (for example, enter="actionName"). They are as follows:

- enter
- escape-press
- focus-in
- focus-out
- insert-newline
- key-press

By providing an action for each of these user events, you trigger actions within your controller or route, which can be used to load data, execute validation, or write to persistent storage. In the next section we'll see how to assign an action to a generic HTML element. But let's spend a bit more time on the {{input}} expression first.

The {{input}} expression can also be used to render a check box by setting the type to checkbox. Similar to the text type, there are a number configurable properties:

- autofocus
- checked
- disabled
- form
- indeterminate
- name
- tabindex

These properties can be bound to a controller property, or not.

Sometimes you'll want to capture more text than you can comfortably display in a text field. In this case, the {{textarea}} expression is available. The {{textarea}} expression works like the {{input}} expression. It renders a control of type textarea, with the value bound to the selected property of the controller's model.

```
{{textarea value=property rows=5 cols=40}}
```

You can also see that we've set a few other HTML properties: rows and cols. As before, if set to controller properties, they'll take the value of these properties; otherwise they'll be set to whatever specific value is provided. In total, the following HTML properties may also be used in the {{textarea}} expression:

| autofocus | cols | disabled | form | maxlength | name |
|---|---|---|---|---|---|
| placeholder | readonly | required | rows | selectionDirection | selectionEnd |
| selectionStart | spellcheck | tabindex | value | wrap | |

These are three of the most fundamental means of linking properties to your user interface. You may think this is limiting, and it would be if this was the only way to create reusable controls in Ember. However, there is another way, and we will see it in the next chapter. Now, let's move on and learn how to enable action handling in Ember.

## Binding Actions to Routes

Your user interface needs to do two things: display data and respond to user input. We've seen the first; now let's start on the second.

Your Route, which has a one-to-one relationship with your template, has a list of functions available to the template called *actions*.

As you might expect, Ember has an expression for linking an HTML element action with the route: the {{action}} expression. Let's look at a basic example of an action, from the login template:

```
<div class="col-md-12">
  Login: {{input value=name}} <button {{action 'login'}}>Login</button>
</div>
```

First, we've added an input field, so the {{action}} will have something to work with. In the route, the action handler takes that value and checks against the server to see if the user is valid. The {{action}} expression is bound to the next control we added: an HTML button that displays the text "Login." Used in this manner, the {{action}} expression binds the login action from the route to the onclick event of the button. The onclick event is the default for the button, which is why the {{action}} expression is bound to this event. When the button is clicked, the login action will fire.

We've already seen a lot on actions in the previous chapter, so this might be a review for you. Let's now take a look at compiling templates.

## Compile Templates

When you create a template in your template.hbs file, the HTML and expression language you add isn't directly built into a string. Beginning with the 1.10 release of Ember, a new template compiler, known as HTMLBars, is used to render your templates. With this compiler, a virtual DOM is created in your application's generated ember-note.js file. So long as you're using Ember CLI to build your application, these details are abstracted away from you.

This form of compilation is important for two reasons. First, a virtual DOM is faster to generate and update than a string-based template, because a virtual DOM can be dealt with at the level of an individual node (for example, a control on a page), versus the entire template being regenerated when a control value changes.

Second, it is this form of compilation that enables Ember to use server-side rendering. Using server-side rendering allows the user to experience a faster initial boot in the application, rather than seeing an empty UI load and waiting for a round-trip to the server to display the app's initial data. Ember's server-side rendering tool, known as FastBoot, is still under development, but promises to expand Ember's capabilities greatly when released.

## Ember Addon: Ember CLI Datepicker

As you've seen, Ember provides a number of basic features for rendering HTML fields using built-in template helpers. However, template helpers are a perfect use case for an Ember addon, and one such addon is Ember CLI Datepicker.

Ember CLI Datepicker is an addon that can be used to add a Bootstrap-styled datepicker control to your web app with a minimum amount of logic. You add this control to your page by adding a single expression, such as the following:

```
{{bootstrap-datepicker placeholder="Choose a date"}}
```

This will insert a text field into your app that, when clicked, pops up a date picker. Choosing a date will add your choice to the text field, allowing your user to quickly enter dates.

Ember CLI Datepicker is just one of several similar addons that you can use to quickly add controls into your app. The site emberobserver.com is a great starting point to find similar addons beyond this single example. We'll continue to see specific addons throughout the book, and discuss how to create your own in Chapter 9, *Building and Using Ember Addons*, on page 121.

The full documentation for Ember CLI Datepicker is available at github.com/soulim/ember-cli-bootstrap-datepicker, along with a link to a demo of how to use the addon.

## Next Steps

You should now have a good handle on the process of building a user interface with Ember and the Handlebars expression language. We saw how templates relate to one another, and we talked quite a bit about the close relationship between templates and routes and using that relationship to render controls. In the next chapter, we'll look at how to take these concepts and create our own reusable controls, known in Ember parlance as *components.*

# CHAPTER 4

# Building In Reuse with Components

The combination of routes and templates is a potent one, and it's responsible for much of the efficiency Ember adds to your development work. But there's an even more powerful feature that we haven't covered yet: components. In Ember, a *component* is a way of extending HTML by creating reusable elements. Similar to the pairing of a route and template, it implements both the user interface and action layer. But components are distinct from routes and templates in that the interface and action layer aren't separable, and a component's scope is isolated to the information passed into the component.

A common use case for components is when you have a segment of your user interface that you want to reuse in multiple places throughout your app. Some examples might be a button, or a menu, or the example we're going to use, a text area with specific logic associated to it.

You may have realized that so far, EmberNote is a bit light on actual notes. We're going to change that now by adding the ability to create notes with real content. To do so, we'll create a new route that relies on a component to drive the editing of the note. This component will implement what you'd expect to see from an edit feature. You'll be able to edit the title and the body of a note and save that note, or close the component and discard your changes.

For added fun, we'll include the ability to use Markdown within the body of your note. Markdown is a lightweight language used to apply basic HTML formatting to plain text. As such, we'll also need the ability to preview the HTML that results from the Markdown process, which we'll do using an Ember addon that we'll retrieve via Ember CLI.

Let's see how to make use of components by creating this new edit feature for EmberNote.

## Create Components

Because a component makes use of a template to define its UI but is itself added to a containing template, the relationship between components and templates can be a bit tricky. It helps me to think of the {{input}} control as an example. It's a stand-alone control that can be used in a generic Ember template. The components you'll define work the same way.

Before we can create our component, we need a place for it to live. We'll create a new route and reference our new component from that route's template. Because we're editing a single note at a time, the most sensible place for this route to live is as a child of the notebooks/notes route.

From a command prompt, run the following Ember CLI command:

```
$ ember generate route notebooks/notes/note --pod
```

This creates an empty stub for the new note route. We'll populate this new class in a moment. First, we need to modify the Router implementation and the notes template to be able to navigate to our new route.

When you created the new route, Ember CLI modified the Router class to include this route at the appropriate place in the hierarchy. Because we're going to query Ember Data for a note record, we'll need to add a parameter to the route to pass the ID of this note to the child route. Open router.js and update it to look like this:

```
ch4/ember-note/app/router.js
import Ember from 'ember';
import config from './config/environment';

var Router = Ember.Router.extend({
  location: config.locationType
});

Router.map(function() {
  this.route('register');
  this.route('login');
  this.route('notebooks', { path:'notebooks/:user_id'}, function() {
    this.route('notes', { path:'notes/:notebook_id'}, function(){
      this.route('note', { path:'note/:note_id'},function(){});
    });
  });
});

export default Router;
```

You'll recall that we use the path attribute in our call to this.route to provide data to the route. The route can use the data from the path attribute however it chooses. We'll want to pass the ID of the current note. Let's tweak the notes template to provide this ID to the route:

```
ch4/ember-note/app/notebooks/notes/template.hbs
<div class="col-md-12">
  Notes
</div>
<div>
  <div class="col-md-4">
    <div>
      title: {{input value=title}} <button {{action 'addNote'}}>Add</button>
    </div>
    <div>
      <ul>
        {{#each model as |note|}}
          <li>
            {{#link-to 'notebooks.notes.note' note.id}}
              {{note.title}}
            {{/link-to}}
            <button {{action 'deleteNote' note}}>delete</button>
          </li>
        {{else}}
          <div>No notes found</div>
        {{/each}}
      </ul>
    </div>
  </div>
  <div class="col-md-8">
    {{outlet}}
  </div>
</div>
```

This changes the notes page from a static list of titles to a list of clickable links. Adding the note.id value to the {{link-to}} expression causes that value to be added into the URL when navigating to the new route. This lets us load the related note record into the child route.

Within our new route, we want to load the related record using Ember Data, and also provide an action that allows us to close the route without saving. We'll see shortly how to make use of these additions. The model hook queries for the note record, and the close action navigates away from the current route by transitioning to the notes route.

Here's our implementation:

```
ch4/ember-note/app/notebooks/notes/note/route.js
import Ember from 'ember';

export default Ember.Route.extend({
  model: function(params) {
    return this.store.findRecord('note', params.note_id);
  },

  actions: {
    close: function() {
      this.transitionTo('notebooks.notes');
    }
  }
});
```

We're now ready to start work on our component.

An Ember *component* is defined by two files. The first is a Handlebars template, which is used to define the user interface of the component. The second is a JavaScript class that extends Ember.Component. This is used to define any action-handling code that the template needs to perform.

We'll call this the edit-note component. As in other areas of Ember, the naming convention is important here. A dash in the name of the component is how Ember identifies it as a component. To create the necessary files using Ember CLI, run the following command at the command prompt:

```
$ ember generate component edit-note --pod
```

Once again, we use the --pod form of the command, as it provides us with a clean project structure. This command creates a directory and two files. The directory is named for the component and resides at the following location: ember-note/app/components/edit-note. This provides us with a single place to go to look for our component definition.

Two files were also created in the edit-note directory: template.hbs and component.js. The first is meant to hold our Handlebars template, and the second is for our component logic.

We now have a few stub files ready to contain our component. Because we want to use it to display a note record, let's take a look now at how to provide data to the component.

## Get Data from Containing Templates

One important distinction between a component and a template/route combination is that a component doesn't have the ability to retrieve its own model. A component relies on the calling template to provide it with the information it needs. This enables component reuse. By being provided the records it will display, a component can be more easily used in a variety of contexts. As long as the records passed to it contain the properties it needs, the component will work just fine. Now, let's see how to define the relationship between a standard, routable template and a component.

When we created the new note route, Ember CLI created not only a route.js file, but also a template.hbs file. While using the --pod form of ember generate commands results in an intuitive project structure, it also results in a raft of files with the same name. It's important to pay attention to your location within the directory tree. So, within the newly created note route, modify the template.hbs file like this:

ch4/ember-note/app/notebooks/notes/note/template.hbs
```
{{edit-note note=model close="close"}}
```

The note template is very terse, as is common with Ember. In this case, the template needs to include just a single expression: our newly defined edit-note component. We're setting two properties on this instance of the component. The note=model assignment is what we use to pass the current model record from the note route into the edit-note component. (We'll discuss the close="close" assignment in *Handle Actions*, on page 57.)

The note=model assignment sets the note's model property as the value of the note property within the edit-note template. As mentioned earlier, Ember components rely on the calling template to set their properties. In this case, we provide the entire record because we want the component to be able to save the record. If this were not the case, we could also have simply passed in the values we wanted to display instead of the entire record.

Now that the edit-note component has a handle on the note it will display, let's take a look at how to create the component user interface.

## Define a Component User Interface

The process of building a component user interface should be familiar to you. For the most part, you use the same set of expressions to build a component interface as you do to build a template. The interface is composed using Handlebars expressions and HTML, and can access any properties defined by the component initialization in the calling template.

As an example, let's take a look at the interface for the edit-note template:

`ch4/ember-note/app/components/edit-note/template.hbs`

```
<div>
  {{input value=note.title}}
  <button {{action "saveNote"}}>save</button>
  <button {{action "closeNote"}}>close</button>
</div>
<div>
  {{textarea rows=10 cols=60 value=note.body}}
</div>
<div>
  {{markdown-to-html markdown=note.body}}
</div>
<div>
  {{yield}}
</div>
```

There's very little about this template that's different from one that's associated to a route. We're accessing the note property, which we set when we added this component to the note template. We use the same Handlebars expressions to display data: the {{input}}) and textarea expressions. These rely on information stored in the note record passed to the component.

## W3C Custom Elements

Ember components are a great idea, and the team deserves a ton of credit for implementing them. As of this writing, there's also an in-progress W3C specification on custom elements, which is very similar to how Ember aims to use components. Rather than wait for the W3C to finalize the specification (which can take a *very* long time), Ember has charged forward with their implementation.

In the W3C specification, a custom element is a developer-defined DOM element that the browser is able to understand and render. It allows developers to define both the user interface and action behavior for the DOM element, just like a component does. This specification, should it be approved, will eventually become a part of the HTML language, which should reduce the need for custom framework support.

The Ember team keeps a close eye on the standards process, so you should feel comfortable that your components will match the specification once it's released, as long as you're keeping relatively current with Ember releases. The in-progress specification is being written on GitHub, and you can read it at any time by going to w3c.github.io/webcomponents/spec/custom/. If you're curious, take a look!

Three other features are demonstrated here: action handling, component nesting, and the {{yield}} tag. We'll take a look at action handling in *Handle Actions*, on page 57. Let's deal with the other two next.

## Nesting Components

A lot of the power of working with Ember components comes from being able to take a combination of HTML tags that occurs repeatedly throughout your app and create a reusable expression that captures that combination. To make that feature even more powerful, Ember components are able to be nested. That is, you can call one component from within another component, and it works as you would expect it to work.

For our new edit-note template, we're already doing this. The reference to {{markdown-to-html markdown=note.body}} is using another component, markdown-to-html. We haven't obtained this component yet, so this reference won't work.

The markdown-to-html component is part of an Ember addon. An *Ember addon* is a library that's useful enough to be shared across multiple applications. It can be made publicly available via npm, like the one we're using, or it can be kept in a private repository. We'll see much more on Ember addons in Chapter 9, *Building and Using Ember Addons*, on page 121.

To install the addon component, run the following command:

```
$ ember install ember-cli-showdown
```

At this point, if your server is running, you may need to press Ctrl-C and then run an ember serve to restart. When you run this command, the EmberNote application is updated to include a dependency on the ember-cli-showdown addon, which includes the markdown-to-html component.[1] The addon is downloaded, along with any needed dependencies, and made available to Ember CLI for build and deployment with the app.

Let's take a look at how we're using this addon. In our template for the edit-note component, we have the following line of code:

```
{{markdown-to-html markdown=note.body}}
```

Just like using an {{input}} expression to create a text field, or using the {{edit-note}} expression to create an edit-note component, we use {{markdown-to-html}} to refer to the markdown-to-html component. The only difference here is that we're nesting one component inside another. So, the only property data we're able to use is property data that's already in the containing component.

The markdown attribute in the previous expression is used to capture the property that the component will use to render HTML. Given a note with a body that's written in Markdown, the component uses the body, applies a

---

1. github.com/gcollazo/ember-cli-showdown, with thanks.

Markdown processor to the body, and renders the resulting HTML. The nested components work well together, as long as you remember to only use properties from the containing scope when building the child component.

Now that you've seen how to combine components via nesting, let's take a look at how a component can allow the calling template to inject content into the component.

## Using the Yield Expression

In the edit-note template we included a {{yield}} expression. This expression allows the calling template to include content into the component. Let's look at a quick example.

In the note template at ember-note/app/notebooks/notes/note/template.hbs, make the following update:

```
{{#edit-note note=model close="close"}}
  Notebook: {{model.notebook.title}}
{{/edit-note}}
```

We've changed the edit-note expression from an inline form to a block form and included a body. This body will be rendered within the component at the location of the {{yield}} tag. However, it is executed by the note template.

This is relevant because it means that you have access to information in a different scope, the scope of the calling template. In this example, because we're passing the entire note model in to the edit-note component, it can see every field in that model. However, if we had passed in just the body of the note object, then that's all it would've been able to see, and only the calling template would've been able to see the full model object.

This notion of scope is also important to think about when designing your actions, as it determines where your action will need to execute, as we'll see shortly. For now, let's take a look at how to tweak the root element your component is wrapped in.

## Altering the Component's Root Element

When you create a component, the HTML generated for that resides inside a root element. By default, Ember uses a <div> tag as the root HTML element. However, in some cases, you may want to wrap your component in a different root element. Any HTML5 element is a valid choice here.

To set the component's root element to something other than <div>, you need to set the tagName property on the component. You can accomplish this in a few ways.

First, it's possible to set the value of this property when you initialize the component in the containing template, like this:

```
{{edit-note note=model close="close" tagName="span"}}
```

This will change the root element of the component to <span>. You can also set the value of the property in the class itself, like this:

```
import Ember from 'ember';

export default Ember.Component.extend({
  tagName: "span"
});
```

This has the same effect as setting the property in the calling template. If you use both mechanisms but set different values, the value set by the calling template wins out.

We've talked a lot about the display concerns related to Ember components. Components are also able to define self-contained action handling code. Let's turn there next.

# Handle Actions

Similar to how a component can render its own content and accept content from the calling template (or component), a component can define its own actions, or it can refer the action back to the calling context.

It's easy to see why this feature exists. In certain cases, such as UI manipulation for the component's UI, you'd prefer not to rely on the calling context, or even allow the calling context to see what you're doing. In other cases, such as navigation, you want the calling context to define the expected behavior.

And there are some use cases that lie in the middle, such as saving a record. If you have passed the entire record into the component, you can save it there. Otherwise, you might have to save it in the calling context.

## Calling Component Actions

When we created our component with Ember CLI, it added a file called ember-note/app/components/edit-note/component.js to our project. This is where we'll define our action handlers.

Open the file, and add the following code:

ch4/ember-note/app/components/edit-note/component.js
```
import Ember from 'ember';

export default Ember.Component.extend({
  actions: {
    saveNote: function() {
      this.get('note').save();
    },
    closeNote: function() {
      this.sendAction('close');
    }
  }
});
```

As you can see, there's not much difference between how we define actions in a component and how we define actions in a route. The actions hash is used to map functions to the names of those functions, just like with a route.

The action function implementations can access any properties that have been passed to the component or injected into the component at the class level. We haven't covered injection yet, and we don't use it here. For now, all you need to know is that it's possible to access certain common objects in various parts of the framework by using injection in some app-wide context.

In this case, the saveNote function is simply responsible for saving the note record. It relies on the fact that the note record comes with its own save logic, and calls that function.

In the template, the following line of code links the saveNote action to the save button:

ch4/ember-note/app/components/edit-note/template.hbs
```
<button {{action "saveNote"}}>save</button>
```

Like with a garden-variety template/route pairing, clicking this button executes the saveNote action.

Component-scoped actions, such as saveNote, have a somewhat more limited use case than referred actions. They can only operate on data that's in the component's scope (that is, data that was passed in by the calling template), or on injected objects. If you're okay being bound by those restrictions, then it's a good idea to keep as much of the component's logic self-contained as possible.

However, if you'd like to defer to the calling route/template to define the actual behavior, you can do that using a *sent action.*

## Sending Actions

Ember components also provide the ability to link the component's template to an action in the calling route, or further up the route hierarchy. A *sent action* is this ability. We'll define one in edit-note.

At first glance, the closeNote action looks no different than the saveNote action. However, rather than executing in the component context, it uses the sendAction method to request that the containing route handle the action. Let's follow this code through the various classes and templates it affects.

First, in the edit-note template, the following code is used to map the action to the close button:

ch4/ember-note/app/components/edit-note/template.hbs
```
<button {{action "closeNote"}}>close</button>
```

This results in the underlying closeNote function being called in the component's action map. That function looks like this:

ch4/ember-note/app/components/edit-note/component.js
```
closeNote: function() {
  this.sendAction('close');
}
```

This is where it gets interesting—and powerful. The sendAction method takes a string parameter, but that string isn't the name of the function that will be called on the containing route. It's actually the value of the component's property, which was set by the containing template, and which points to the function on the containing route. Here's what the containing template looks like:

ch4/ember-note/app/notebooks/notes/note/template.hbs
```
{{edit-note note=model close="close"}}
```

On the left side of the close="close" assignment, we define the name of the component parameter we'll use to hold the action. This matches the string passed to sendAction in the closeNote action. On the right side of the assignment, we use the name of the action in the route. The underlying route should look like this:

ch4/ember-note/app/notebooks/notes/note/route.js
```
import Ember from 'ember';

export default Ember.Route.extend({
  model: function(params) {
    return this.store.findRecord('note', params.note_id);
  },
```

```
  actions: {
    close: function() {
      this.transitionTo('notebooks.notes');
    }
  }
});
```

You see the close action defined here. In this case, it defines a simple route transition, with the effect of moving one step upward in the route hierarchy, and closing out the edit-note screen in the process.

As mentioned earlier, this is a very powerful construct. In essence, sendAction allows you to define a component with placeholder actions, the exact result of which can be determined by the containing route. This adds greatly to the reuse of components, because it allows them to be used in different contexts but still describe part of the behavior, while allowing the calling context to fill in the details.

The sendAction method has one other wrinkle. If you call sendAction without passing a string parameter indicating the name of the property, the method assumes you're looking for an action defined with the property name action, and acts accordingly. This might be useful in cases when a component is likely to have just one associated action, but I prefer the named property form of the method, as I think it adds clarity.

As we've seen, components are able to respond to actions either by defining the behavior explicitly within the component or by referring the action to the component's calling context. You'll use both of these, depending on your needs. Before we wrap up our discussion on components, let's take a look at one more way for a component to respond to user events.

## Listening for Events

Using an action to respond to events is a simple way to link logic to a component. It's also possible to execute code in an event-driven manner.

In Ember every component is based on the Ember.View class, even the ones like {{input}} that ship with the framework. We haven't touched on views because they aren't a concept you need to know to build apps with Ember. They're important mainly if you're developing the Ember framework.

In this case, though, knowing about views is helpful. Because each component is based on a view, you can respond to any event that a view can respond to. For instance, if you're designing a stateful <div> tag, you might want to handle the click event, and change the state of your <div> when the click occurs, like this:

```
import Ember from 'ember';

export default Ember.Component.extend({
  click: function(event) {
    //Change the state here
  }
});
```

This offers you another means of responding to user input in your component. By relying on the view, you gain access to a variety of events, which are too numerous to list here.[2]

## Ember Addon: Ember CLI Materialize

Components are all about taking a commonly used snippet of HTML from your app, extracting it into a separate object, and reusing that object throughout. When you add a CSS stylesheet to that model, you can create a coherent set of user interface elements that follow a standardized design.

Google's Material Design spec (found at www.google.com/design/spec/material-design/introduction.html) is one such standardized design, but how do you use such a set of principles in Ember?

The Ember CLI Materialize addon is a project that attempts to answer that question. It is both an Ember CLI wrapper for the Materialize CSS framework and a library of related components. By including Ember CLI Materialize in your project, you can take advantage of the stylesheet and components to jump-start the design of your application, and extend it as needed.

The full documentation for Ember CLI Materialize can be found at github.com/sgasser/ember-cli-materialize, along with a link to a demo site demonstrating the addon and its components.

## Next Steps

In Ember 2, components are an increasingly important part of the framework. By combining the ideas behind templates and routes in a self-contained, reusable manner, they allow you to create your own set of controls that can be applied to common problems throughout the app. Now that we've seen components, we've touched on most of the major aspects of the user interface layer of Ember. It's time now to turn to the data layer and learn how Ember works with RESTful services using Ember Data.

---

2. Check out http://emberjs.com/api/classes/Ember.View.html#toc_event-names for the full list of events.

# CHAPTER 5

# Modeling Your Data

Ember has a lot to offer as a front-end web framework. So far, we've focused almost entirely on your app's rendering and navigation. But as you build apps, you'll eventually want to include data. Ember has a solution for that: Ember Data.

*Ember Data* packs many things into one small library. It offers your web client a straightforward modeling approach to include simple records in your app. It reads from RESTful services, caches the data it loads, and persists these records back to the server.

In this chapter you'll learn how to use Ember Data to access data from a RESTful service. We'll focus on an optimally designed RESTful service that requires little to no configuration from our app. By looking at all of the data-related code we've added to EmberNote so far, you'll see how Ember Data works. Let's start by looking at the model classes we've created so far.

## Define Your Models

An Ember Data model class represents a record in some sort of persistent storage. Because we're working on the web, it's likely that this persistent storage is accessed via a RESTful API. An Ember Data record is an instance of a model class that actually holds data; a model is simply the definition of that record. The most important thing about a record is the data it maintains. Let's look at how to define what data is maintained by a record.

### Defining a Model's Fields

As with each of the other classes we've created, we define models by first running an Ember CLI command to get a stub version of the class. In *Adding a Data Service*, on page 12, we ran the following command to generate our User model class.

```
$ ember generate model user
```

The stub version of this class had no fields. We'll add them so that our class looks like this:

ch5/ember-note/app/models/user.js
```
import DS from 'ember-data';

export default DS.Model.extend({
  name: DS.attr('string')
});
```

With Ember Data, your model definition is very simple. Your model has a set of fields that you define as key-value pairs in your class. The key is how you will reference the data from within your templates (that is, user.name).

When you define a field, you have a few options for defining the field type. If you're adding a field to hold a single value, you'll use DS.attr. Calling this function creates a field in your model. Call this function with no parameters, and the model will simply accept whatever data type is passed to it.

Alternatively, you can give it a type, known as a Transform, and Ember Data will take the raw data provided by your API and try to make it fit the type you provide. That's what our user.js example does. Ember Data offers four available default choices: string, number, Boolean, and date. If needed, you can define your own Transform implementations, but we'll get by with the basics for now.

You can also define a default value for your field. For example, if your call to DS.attr looks like this:

```
name: DS.attr("string", {defaultValue: "Matt"})
```

the value Matt will be used if a given record doesn't have a value for name.

## Defining Model Relationships

Your model classes might have fields that contain a record, or even a list of records, rather than a basic data type. Ember Data makes this possible through the use of two constructs: DS.hasMany and DS.belongsTo. To see an example of this, let's look at the notebook.js file:

ch5/ember-note/app/models/notebook.js
```
import DS from 'ember-data';

export default DS.Model.extend({
  title: DS.attr('string'),
  user: DS.belongsTo('user'),
  notes: DS.hasMany('note')
});
```

Both the hasMany and belongsTo functions define a relationship between the calling class and another model definition. The argument to this function is the name of the other model's class. In the notebook model example, we reference the user model from our belongsTo function and the note model from our hasMany function. Semantically, this makes sense: a notebook belongs to a user and has many notes.

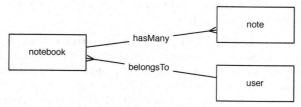

It is often desirable to traverse model relationships in both directions. For example, from the perspective of the note, you could include a belongsTo relationship back to the notebook. And from the user, you could include a hasMany relationship to the notebook.

Of course, the cardinality of model relationships isn't always a one-to-many or a many-to-one. If you want a one-to-one relationship, simply create both relationships using belongsTo. For a many-to-many, both sides should be a hasMany.

Now that you have a better understanding of how to define a model class, you'll need to learn how to populate them. Let's take a look at how to load data from a server.

## Load Data from RESTful Services

When using Ember to build your apps, it's very likely that your data will come from a RESTful service. A RESTful service uses HTTP as a data query and delivery mechanism. Based on HTTP requests, it can be used to return data to the calling logic, or to modify a data store in some manner.

The Ember project is very keen on adapting the best ideas from the web community into the Ember framework, and Ember Data's use of RESTful services is no exception. By simply declaring your model class, you are able to use the DS.Store object to get data from your server, assuming that the RESTful service exposes the expected API.

Although we won't dig too deeply into the implementation of a RESTful service, throughout the rest of the chapter we'll note the URL to which Ember Data makes requests. In *Use Serializers to Access Legacy APIs*, on page 82, we'll cover how to use Ember Data to access APIs that don't follow the expected conventions.

## RESTful APIs

As with many notions in the programming world, there's some debate over what constitutes a RESTful API. (Often this takes the form of "Your API isn't RESTful!" "No, YOUR API isn't RESTful!") Leaving all of that aside, let's talk about how RESTful APIs are meant to be used with Ember Data.

Generally speaking, a RESTful service is a means of using a uniform resource identifier to access data and execute functions. RESTful services often, but not always, use HTTP as a transport protocol. Each unique URI and verb combination defines an action and the related record (or set of records) to use when applying that action. For example, if you want to get the note record with id 24, you can make a GET request of /note/24 and expect to get the current state of the record, if it exists.

The implementation of a RESTful API is beyond the scope of this book, with the exception of the mock services we've been creating (and don't use these in a production environment, please). You might use any number of technologies to implement one, such as Ruby on Rails, Node.js, Java, or .NET. The choice is yours.

Once you've defined a model class, you'll want to be able to load data from that class's API endpoint. Before you can do that, your app will need to declare an instance of the DS.RESTAdapter class. Let's look at the one we declared for the EmberNote project:

```
ch5/ember-note/app/adapters/application.js
import DS from 'ember-data';

export default DS.RESTAdapter.extend({
  namespace: 'api'
});
```

This adapter is as terse as it gets. The single function of this implementation of RESTAdapter is to identify the API's root URL. In general, an adapter is able to be responsible for much more than this, but we'll start with a simple one for now and cover adapters in greater detail in *Adapt to a Nonconventional API*, on page 77.

With this adapter in place, we're ready to begin querying the API for records.

## Querying the API

When we first began working with Ember Data, we used it to display a list of notebooks that the logged-on user owned. As you can see from our definition, each notebook record belongs to one user:

```
ch5/ember-note/app/models/notebook.js
import DS from 'ember-data';

export default DS.Model.extend({
  title: DS.attr('string'),
  user: DS.belongsTo('user'),
  notes: DS.hasMany('note')
});
```

Given that model, we used the model hook of the notebooks route to load data from the API:

```
ch5/ember-note/app/notebooks/route.js
import Ember from 'ember';

export default Ember.Route.extend({
  model: function(params) {
    return this.store.query('notebook',{user: params.user_id});
  },
  actions: {
    addNotebook: function() {
      var notebook = this.store.createRecord('notebook', {
        title: this.controller.get('title'),
        user: this.controllerFor('application').get('user')
      });
      notebook.save().then(() => {
        console.log('save successful');
        this.controller.set('title',null);
        this.refresh();
      }, function() {
        console.log('save failed');
      });
    }
  }

});
```

As you'll recall from *Set Your Model*, on page 23, the model hook is used to obtain the data that will be displayed for a given route. We use the this.store object to find data within the route. The store object is an instance of DS.Store, which is the client-side data persistence store.

The find function typically takes two parameters. The first is the class name for the data type that the find function will return. The second is a list of parameters to query against. If this list is blank, all records of that type should be returned by the API. In our case, we provide the ID of the currently logged-in user, so all notebooks returned will belong to that user. This list of parameters can contain multiple values, and if it does, the API is expected to return all records that match each of the criteria provided.

If you don't know the ID of a record you want to load, you can write queries using the contents of other fields. That's the query form we're using in route.js, when we call this.store.query('notebook',{user: params.user_id}) to find the notebooks that belong to a certain user. The user's ID is a known piece of information about the notebook, but it doesn't uniquely identify the notebook. However, if you do know the record's ID, like in our edit-note example from the previous chapter, then there's another form of the find function you can use:

```
model: function(params) {
  return this.store.findRecord("note",params.id);
}
```

The biggest difference is that in this form, we're not defining which field to search. Ember Data assumes that we're searching the id field of the given record. If you want to load all records, you simply call findAll with no parameters, like this:

```
this.store.findAll("note");
```

The different forms of querying your API result in slightly different HTTP requests to your back end. The query form creates a GET request to your API that uses URL query parameters to communicate the query to the back end. For example, this.store.query("notebook", { user: 1}) will result in this request: GET "/api/notebooks?user=1". The id-based form also creates a GET request. For example, this.store.findRecord("note",1) results in GET "api/note/1".

These URLs are the default URLs generated by Ember Data. However, if your server API doesn't match what Ember Data generates, you don't need to change your server. In *Allow the Adapter to Query a Nonconventional API*, on page 85, we'll see how to use Ember Data to alter the URLs it queries against to match an existing API. This is one of the many ways Ember Data makes it easy to consume a RESTful API. Another is browser-based caching, which we'll look at now.

## Using the Store

If all the DS.Store object did was to proxy access to a RESTful API, it would still be useful. But it also provides a browser-based cache of the data loaded since your user's session began. Once a record is loaded by a user via the find methods described in the previous section, that record resides in the cache, providing faster access to it.

We've worked with the store variable already to find records, but we haven't really discussed what it is. The store is your primary resource for interacting with RESTful APIs. In addition to providing the find methods, it caches the data returned by those methods and provides methods for working with the cached data. It also provides methods for modifying records, as we'll see later in this chapter. An instance of DS.Store, as represented by the store variable, is available in every instance of Ember.Route.

Ember Data provides a variety of methods for working with data once it has been loaded into the store. To begin with, if you want to get all records of a certain type that are already in the store, it provides the peekAll method:

```
var allNotes = this.store.peekAll("note");
```

This method returns an array of all note records that are currently in the store. Whenever you call a query method of any of the varieties described earlier, the results are loaded into the store and available throughout the app.

When working with a browser-side cache, you'll need to be aware of scenarios when other users may have modified cached data. The store isn't kept up to date with each change as it occurs, so it's a good idea to reload records from the server when you need to use them, if they are able to be modified by others. To do this, Ember Data provides the reload flag for findRecord and findAll. For example, if we want to make sure we have the most recent changes to a shared note record when we load our route, we would call the following:

```
model: function(params) {
  this.store.findRecord("note",params.id,{ reload:true })
}
```

Using reload:true will always ensure that you get the record from the server and include the most recent changes.

There's a second way to accomplish this, assuming you have a handle on the record. If a record has already been loaded in the cache, findRecord calls the reload method on the record instance. If you already have the record, you can do the following to refresh this object from the server:

```
record.reload();
```

DS.Store also contains a method to pull all records of a given type from the server, regardless of cache state. To do this, call the findAll method with reload:true:

```
model: function(params) {
  this.store.findAll("note",{ reload:true });
}
```

You may be thinking that the only way to guarantee you have the most recent data is to use the reload parameter. This is partially true, because the findRecord and findAll methods will return records already cached in the store, if any exist. However, DS.Store provides a way to evict all records of a given type from the store:

```
model: function(param) {
  // Before looking for my data, flush the cache
  this.store.unloadAll("note");
  // Now get my records
  return this.store.query("note",{notebook: param.notebook_id});
}
```

Calling unloadAll will result in a clean slate for the following query method to work with. This is useful when you want to be able to execute named-parameter queries against the store, while making sure that the results it returns are the most recent data from the server.

DS.Store has a number of methods for working with server APIs and for storing results of API calls in a browser-resident repository. As you'd expect, it also provides a number of ways of dealing with those records once they've been loaded. In the next section we'll look at how to use Ember Data to use the records we get from the API.

# Work with Records

While many of the methods in the DS.Store class deal with loading and caching lists of records, your app will also often work with records directly. Sometimes you'll use the store, and sometimes you'll call methods on the record itself. Let's start with one that we call from the store, and learn how we can add data with the Ember app.

## Creating Records

For users to find your app useful, they need to be able to add data to persistent storage. We've seen this already in the EmberNote application, where users add their own notebooks and notes. Let's take a look at that code now. In the notebooks route, we added a feature that let users add a notebook:

```
ch5/ember-note/app/notebooks/route.js
addNotebook: function() {
  var notebook = this.store.createRecord('notebook', {
    title: this.controller.get('title'),
    user: this.controllerFor('application').get('user')
  });
  notebook.save().then(() => {
    console.log('save successful');
    this.controller.set('title',null);
    this.refresh();
```

```
  }, function() {
    console.log('save failed');
  });
}
```

The new notebook is created in the store by the following code: var notebook = this.store.createRecord('notebook', {...});. The createRecord method takes two parameters. The first parameter is the model type of the record you want to create. In this case it's a notebook type. The second parameter is a properties list, consisting of a set of key-value pairs. The keys should match the names of attributes as defined in the referenced model implementation. The values are then set as the value of each attribute. In this case we're pulling the values out of fields in our controller and using them to populate the new record.

---

**Saving New Records**

 It's important to realize that calling createRecord does not result in the new record being written to persistent storage. This new record lives only in the store until the next block of code is called. To write this new record to persistent storage, you must call the save method on the desired record.

---

The save method returns a Promise, which can resolve to either success or failure. The then method on the resulting Promise object is called once the Promise has resolved. As the logging statements demonstrate, the first argument to then is executed when the Promise resolves successfully, and the second when it does not. This allows you to handle each case separately and keep the user informed of your progress.

When the save method is called, the store prepares a request to the RESTful API in the form of an HTTP POST request. The body of the request contains all of the information necessary to create the record within persistent storage. For example, if we wanted to create a note with a title of "new note," a description of "description," and belonging to notebook 12, the request would look something like this:

```
POST /api/notes
{note: {title: "new note", body: "description", notebook: "12"}}
```

---

**Monitoring Request/Response Traffic**

 As you're working through these examples, it can be helpful to keep an eye on the request/response traffic. Chrome, Firefox, Safari, and Internet Explorer all have built-in developer tools that allow you to observe the traffic a site generates. This is very useful in investigating the Ember Data requests further.

Observe that there are no request parameters for this request. We're simply POSTing to a generic URL for the model type: /api/notes. The POST method for this URL is reserved for receiving requests that relate exclusively to the creation of new records, and it's not used for update requests, which use the PUT method.

Now that we've seen how to add new records to Ember apps, let's look at how to modify existing records.

## Updating Records

There's not much difference between how you create a record and how you update one: you call the save method on a record that has the data you want to save. The big difference comes in how Ember Data translates the action into an HTTP request.

When a save is called on a record that already exists in persistent storage, this results in an HTTP PUT request to the API. For example, in the edit-note route, we used the following action to save changes:

```
ch4/ember-note/app/components/edit-note/component.js
import Ember from 'ember';

export default Ember.Component.extend({
  actions: {
    saveNote: function() {
      this.get('note').save();
    },
    closeNote: function() {
      this.sendAction('close');
    }
  }
});
```

The note record, when saved, results in an HTTP request that looks something like this:

```
PUT "/api/notes/12"
{note: {title: "edited note", body: "edited description", notebook: "12"}}
```

There are similarities to the HTTP POST request generated for a new record. Each request contains a JSON representation of the record to be saved. Each record uses the same endpoint, /api/notes. However, the save method uses the PUT verb when it's aware of an existing record, and to identify the record, it adds a path segment to the URL that contains the value of the id field from the record. From this request, the API is expected to save changes to the record as provided by the request.

## Deleting Records

Of course, your users will sometimes make mistakes, or want to let data go. For this, you'll want to let them delete records. Ember Data provides two different ways to accomplish this. The first is similar to the methods we've seen thus far. Let's build out EmberNote a bit, to allow users to delete notes from within the notebooks/notes route. Let's start by adding a delete button to the list of notes. Make sure the template looks like this:

```
ch5/ember-note/app/notebooks/notes/template.hbs
<div class="col-md-12">
  Notes
</div>
<div>
  <div class="col-md-4">
    <div>
      title: {{input value=title}} <button {{action 'addNote'}}>Add</button>
    </div>
    <div>
      <ul>
        {{#each model as |note|}}
          <li>
            {{#link-to 'notebooks.notes.note' note.id}}
              {{note.title}}
            {{/link-to}}
            <button {{action 'deleteNote' note}}>delete</button>
          </li>
        {{else}}
          <div>No notes found</div>
        {{/each}}
      </ul>
    </div>
  </div>
  <div class="col-md-8">
    {{outlet}}
  </div>
</div>
```

Now let's alter the route to define the action referenced from the new button. Add the following action:

```
ch5/ember-note/app/notebooks/notes/route.js
deleteNote: function(note) {
  console.log('deleting note with title ' + note.get('title'));
  note.deleteRecord();
  note.save();
}
```

The call to deleteRecord doesn't fully delete it from the back end. As you see, you also need to call save for the record to be fully deleted.

As with the other methods, save results in an HTTP request to the API, this time a delete request:

```
DELETE "/api/notes/12"
```

Because we're deleting the record, we don't need to provide any further information beyond the ID in the URL. The API knows all it needs to know and returns success or failure.

Unlike the other operations, though, deletion has a shortcut form as well. The destoryRecord method will delete the record from the server without a need to call save first. My preference is to emphasize readability and familiar-looking code, so I tend to prefer the deleteRecord form, but this option is there.

Let's take a look now at how to determine a record's state, which can help you decide what, if anything, needs to be done with it.

## Getting a Record's State

We've been building EmberNote to be action-driven in regard to saving records, but you may occasionally want to save records as a background process. In this pattern, you'll want to use the record's state to determine which records to save. To get the state of a record, you call the following:

```
var state = record.get('currentState.stateName');
```

The state of the record can take one of the following values:

- root.deleted.saved

- root.deleted.uncommitted

- root.deleted.inFlight

- root.empty

- root.loaded.created.uncommitted

- root.loaded.created.inFlight

- root.loaded.saved

- root.loaded.updated.uncommitted

- root.loaded.updated.inFlight

- root.loading

In general, these states are fairly self-explantory, but the following nuances are worth mentioning: *uncommitted* means that a record has not been saved to persistent storage, *inFlight* means that a save is in process (recall that saves are asynchronous), and *saved* means a record has been saved to persistent storage.

By getting a list of all records in the store, it's possible to run a background save process on an interval basis and have data saved without requiring user action.

## Purging Records From the Store

There may also be times when you want to eject records from the store without saving them. Consider the case where a user is navigating away from a record without having changed data. You can keep the record loaded into the cache, and it will be there when you need it later. Or, if you're interested in limiting the size of your cache, or in discarding unsaved changes, you may want to eject the record. To do this, call the following:

```
if(record.hasDirtyAttributes()) {
  record.rollbackAttributes();
}
this.store.unloadRecord(record);
```

The method unloadRecord is used to remove records from the store. However, you'll note that we checked the state of the record before unloading it using hasDirtyAttributes. This determines whether the record has changes that require a save. The unloadRecord method will not remove a dirty object from the cache, so we use the rollbackAttributes method first to discard changes, and then we can drop the record from the store. As of this writing, this is the only way to discard records from the cache; the cache itself does not discard records based on aging.

### Ember Addon: Fireplace

Perhaps you'd like to totally avoid creating your own back end. If that's the case, you might be interested in Firebase, and an Ember addon known as Fireplace.

Firebase is an API-as-a-Service provider that you can use to host a custom API that you define. Hosted at www.firebase.com, this commercial product lets you quickly spin up an API that you can use in a JavaScript, iOS, or Android app.

While Firebase is a cool product, the Ember addon is what I find really interesting. This addon, maintained at github.com/rlivsey/fireplace and documented at http://livsey.org/fireplace/, wraps the Firebase JavaScript client in an Ember addon, and exposes the features of Firebase to your app via an Ember Data store. By simply signing up at Firebase and dropping this addon into your project, you can easily get up and running with a full back-end API.

## Next Steps

Ember Data can be quite helpful when working with RESTful APIs. As we've seen, it offers a robust feature set for dealing with data that you obtain from such a server. However, we've only covered the easy part of the story. You may often need to deal with an API that, for one reason or another, doesn't follow the conventions Ember Data expects. There's no need to give up on Ember Data if you find out your API doesn't conform to its expectations. This is why, despite being focused primarily on the front end, it's important to understand the HTTP traffic Ember Data generates. In the next chapter, you'll learn about a few Ember Data features that allow you to work with an API that follows its own rules, and about how to make such APIs do what you want them to do.

# CHAPTER 6

# Reading Nonstandard APIs

One of the core principles of Ember is to value convention over configuration. As such, Ember Data is quite easy to use with a RESTful API that uses the conventions discussed in *Work with Records*, on page 70. However, at some point you'll almost certainly come into contact with an API that doesn't follow these conventions.

To help with this, Ember Data has a series of classes that adapt nonstandard APIs to follow the conventions the rest of Ember expects. This can be as simple as translating attribute names from one naming convention to another, or as complicated as using Ember Data to alter JSON in flight.

In this chapter, we'll take a look at how to use Ember Data to work with any standard or nonstandard API you might encounter.

## Adapt to a Nonconventional API

As built so far, the EmberNote API has used the conventions Ember Data expects from an API. In this chapter, we'll first create a parallel version of the EmberNote API that doesn't follow the traditional conventions. Then, we'll use the new version to learn how to make Ember Data fit such an API.

To start this process, you'll want to create a copy of each of the mock server files we've created. Take each file in the ember-note/server/mocks directory, copy it, and append -alt-api to the end of the filename, before the file extension, so notes.js becomes notes-alt-api.js. Don't forget to leave the original files in place. In each of the -alt-api files, where we're creating the NEDB data file, change the name of the data file by appending -alt to the name, like this:

```
var noteDB = new nedb({ filename : 'notes-alt', autoload: true});
```

Then, at the bottom of each of the new files, change the listener URL to include a path segment for api:

```
app.use('/api/alt/notes', notesRouter);
```

Run the ember serve command to ensure your app starts with the new API.

## Adding Request Headers to Your API

With this new API running, let's modify RESTAdapter as follows:

```
ch6/ember-note/app/adapters/application.js
import DS from 'ember-data';

export default DS.RESTAdapter.extend({
  namespace: 'api/alt',
});
```

This simple change to namespace will cause the adapter to send requests to the alternate API endpoints. If you load EmberNote in a browser now, you'll see that your previously registered user isn't able to log in because we created new underlying data stores. In a production app you wouldn't need to do this, but because our mock server endpoints all run within the same Node instance, we had to create separate data stores to work around a limitation on loading the same store twice with NEDB.

Beyond just setting the API endpoint path, there are a few other customization options available for RESTAdapter. For example, many APIs require HTTP request headers to identify the user. RESTAdapter contains a property called headers that you can set as needed. Let's modify EmberNote to add a user token as a header on each request once the user has logged in.

To populate the headers from within our RESTAdapter, we need a way to provide user data to the adapter. This user data is available within the login route when a user first signs in. Previously, when we wanted to get at user data outside of the user route, we simply used the controllerFor method. However, this method isn't available inside our RESTAdapter. To get at the user information from the adapter, we're going to need to use one of the advanced features of Ember: dependency injection. We've used dependency injection previously—in fact, whenever we've called this.store in a route or controller. Let's see how to create our own objects for use with dependency injection.

### Creating and Injecting a User Session

We're going to create a class, called Session, and use it to store information we want to share between classes. We'll use an initializer to initialize this class and make it available. An initializer is a function that runs when an Ember application is first started in the browser, and it's very useful in making objects available via dependency injection. To create one, run the following Ember CLI command from the EmberNote root:

```
$ ember generate initializer session
```

This command generates a stub for your initializer. Add the following code to the stub to complete the initializer:

ch6/ember-note/app/initializers/session.js

```
import Ember from 'ember';

export function initialize(container,application) {
    var session = Ember.Object.extend();
    application.register('session:main', session);
    application.inject('adapter', 'session', 'session:main');
    application.inject('route','session','session:main');
}

export default {
  name: 'session',
  initialize: initialize
};
```

The first block of code defines the initialize method for this initializer. The method takes the app's container and application instances. Within the method, we extend the Ember.Object and assign the result to a variable called session. We'll use this anonymous class to hold our session information using the get and set methods on Ember.Object.

Now that we have a session object, we need to make it available to types that need it. First, we register this instance with the application object under the name "session:main". Using the register method results in a single instance of the session object being created and shared across the app. We can then use this single instance to share data between objects that would otherwise be unable to do so.

With the object registered, the next two lines of code inject this object into the type factories for the adapter and route types. The first parameter to the inject function is the type we want to inject into. The second parameter is the property name we want to make the object available under within that type, and the third parameter is the name we registered the object under previously. The remaining code in the initializer is used to help organize the execution order, as we'll see in the next chapter.

Now that we have an initializer ready to store the session, let's modify the login route to use it:

## Ember Addon: Ember CLI Simple Auth

Our example session object is a good start, but we're likely to need more sophisticated authentication and session management at some point. Ember itself doesn't provide a session object or built-in authentication mechanism, but like with most other things, there's an addon for that. Let's take a quick look at Ember Simple Auth and the Ember CLI Simple Auth addon.

The Ember Simple Auth project is a library for adding authentication to an Ember app. Among other things, it allows you to authenticate against either your own server or external services that support OAuth. Once authenticated, you can use Ember Simple Auth to authorize requests to your server, protecting actions by preventing unauthorized users from reaching them.

Ember Simple Auth isn't an addon by itself, however. To use it with Ember CLI, you need the Ember CLI Simple Auth addon, which packages the Ember Simple Auth code and makes it able to be installed from Ember CLI. This is a good example of how Ember CLI makes it possible to share good ideas. A codebase such as Ember Simple Auth becomes as easy to get as a single command within your project.

The full documentation for the Ember CLI Simple Auth addon is at github.com/simplabs/ember-cli-simple-auth.

ch6/ember-note/app/login/route.js
```js
import Ember from 'ember';

export default Ember.Route.extend({
  actions: {
    login: function() {
      this.store.query('user', {
        name: this.controller.get('name')
      }).then((users) => {
        if(users.get('length') === 1) {
          var user = users.objectAt(0);
          this.session.set('user',user);
          this.transitionTo('notebooks', user.get('id'));
        }
        else {
          console.log('unexpected query result');
        }
      });
    }
  }
});
```

Because we injected the session object into the route type, every route in our application now has a variable called session. We'll use this variable to store the logged-on user so we can reference it in RESTAdapter, which we'll now update as follows:

```
ch6/ember-note/app/adapters/application.js
import DS from 'ember-data';

export default DS.RESTAdapter.extend({
  namespace: 'api/alt',
  headers: function() {
    if(this.get('session.user')) {
      return {
        'username' : this.get('session.user').get('name')
      };
    }
  }.property('session.user')
});
```

This new block of code adds a list of key-value pairs as HTTP request headers to each request that is issued by RESTAdapter. In this case, we add just one header: "username". The if statement ensures that we only add this header if the user has logged on. We're using Ember's notion of a computed property to set the header. A computed property takes the result of a function and assigns it to the property. The property function passes any required dependencies to the function—in this case we need the session.user object. We set the "username" header to the "name" field from the logged-on user object. This ensures that each HTTP request from our adapter will have this header, which can be used for API keys, user authentication/authorization, and so forth.

This is just one possible way to use dependency injection, a topic we cover in more detail in Chapter 7, *Reusing Code in Ember*, on page 91.

## Adding a Custom API Hostname

It took a bit of work to get there, but using initializers, injection, and a session object to provide header data to RESTAdapter was a good demonstration of how extensible Ember is. We'll see more on this in the next chapter.

In addition to the properties we've covered, the RESTAdapter also allows you to customize the hostname used for the API call, like this:

```
export default DS.RESTAdapter.extend({
  hostname: 'https://embernote.example.com'
}
```

This is useful in cases when your API might reside on a different subdomain from your Ember code.

Now that we've seen a good deal of how to customize your adapters, let's take a look at how to translate an idiosyncratic API into the conventions Ember Data model classes expect, by making use of RESTSerializer.

# Use Serializers to Access Legacy APIs

As much as we might hope to leave them behind, sometimes we need to work with a legacy API. We don't have to throw out our entire model layer, though. By making use of RESTSerializer, we can take the raw data returned by this API and get it into the form we expect.

With Ember Data, a *serializer* is a class that takes a block of data and translates it into a different form for storage in an external context. For example, a serializer can be used to modify attribute names to match your expected format. You can take a raw JSON payload and alter its structure to match your model layer or remove extraneous information. And you can serialize your model data back into the format the servers expects and save it.

---

**RESTful Calls from Ember Data**

 It's important to keep in mind that while you can change many things about the JSON payloads that move back and forth—and even alter the expected name of your endpoint as we'll see shortly —you're still using the same HTTP verbs to interrogate your API. With RESTAdapter and RESTSerializer, you can change a lot, but your API is still subject to the same conventions in that regard.

---

Now that we have a parallel API, let's mess with it a bit more to learn how to use these features. Let's start by implementing the serialize and normalize methods.

### Serializing Data

Let's make a change to how the notebook data type is written to the database. We'll create a per-type serializer for the notebook class, so that only this data type is impacted by the changes. Run the following Ember CLI command to create this new serializer:

```
$ ember generate serializer notebook
```

This command creates an empty stub class. Now, let's assume that this alternate notebook endpoint uses a slightly different capitalization format for data attributes: it uses a class-like capitalization format. For example, instead of "title", the field will be known as "Title".

Classes that extend RESTSerializer are used to make changes to data that is obtained from or sent to the server. Our alternate API uses a different capitalization scheme. Within the notebook model class, the attributes are camelcased. Our API expects records to be stored in class-cased attributes. So, when a record is saved, the conventional model attribute names need to be converted from camel-case to class-case. Take a look at the serialize method:

```
ch6/ember-note/app/serializers/notebook.js
import DS from 'ember-data';

export default DS.RESTSerializer.extend({
  normalize: function(typeClass, hash, prop) {
    hash.title = hash.Title;
    delete hash.Title;
    hash.user = hash.User;
    delete hash.User;
    return this._super(typeClass, hash, prop);
  },
  serialize: function(snapshot, options) {
    var json = {
      Title: snapshot.attr('title'),
      User: snapshot.belongsTo('user').id
    };
    return json;
  },
});
```

The serialize method is used to modify records on their way to the server. If you implement this method in your RESTSerializer implementation, you can control the JSON body of your HTTP request to match your API's expectations. Both new records and changes to records will funnel through this method. The snapshot parameter represents a model record at the time the serialize method is called. The options parameter contains a hash with one attribute: includeId. This attribute will be set by the calling adapter. When you're creating a new record, this will be set to true, otherwise false.

Our serialize method creates a JSON hash, but alters the keys by replacing the camel-cased keys with class-cased keys. The values stay the same. At present, our API endpoint determines the value of the id field, so we don't need to worry about it.

Earlier in this chapter, we changed how we store the user object so that we store it in a session. As a result, we need to make one minor change to the notebooks route to use the session object. Update the addNotebook action to the following:

```
ch6/ember-note/app/notebooks/route.js
import Ember from 'ember';

export default Ember.Route.extend({
  model: function(params) {
    return this.store.query('notebook',{user: params.user_id});
  },
  actions: {
      addNotebook: function() {
        var notebook = this.store.createRecord('notebook', {
          title: this.controller.get('title'),
          user: this.session.get('user') //Changed this from controllerFor
        });
        notebook.save().then(() => {
          console.log('save successful');
          this.controller.set('title',null);
          this.refresh();
        }, function() {
          console.log('save failed');
        });
      }
  }
});
```

This change allows us to use the user record stored in the session when we save a new notebook.

If the serialize method takes data from Ember Data's expected format and converts it so the API can consume it, the normalize method does the opposite. We're already making use of this in our RESTSerializer. Let's see how.

## Normalizing Data

The normalize method is defined in the base implementation of RESTSerializer. It is this implementation that we rely on. Because we're performing a fairly straightforward normalization of our data and changing the case of the keys, all we need to do is define this function. Let's look again at the code:

```
normalize: function(typeClass, hash, prop) {
  hash.title = hash.Title;
  delete hash.Title;
  hash.user = hash.User;
  delete hash.User;
  return this._super(typeClass, hash, prop);
}
```

This function is simple: it maps the values held in class-cased keys onto the corresponding camel-cased keys, then deletes the class-cased entries.

At times there may be other work that you want to do in the normalize function, such as deleting unnecessary data points or adding new data. The following assigns a property in your payload with the current time.

```
normalize: function(type, hash, prop) {
  hash['currentTime'] = new Date();
  this._super(type, hash, prop);
}
```

These parameters represent the data type (that is, the model class), the name of the hash key to use (such as "notebooks" in our previous example), and the payload returned from the server. It's important to remember to call this._super with the parameters to ensure that the superclass normalize method is called and your defined normalizeHash operations are run.

## Allow the Adapter to Query a Nonconventional API

At this point, the changes you've made to the serializer will let you save into the new API's format, but you won't be able to query data. Before you can query, you need to create a new RESTAdapter for your notebook model. To begin, run the following command:

```
$ ember generate adapter notebook
```

This creates a stub class at ember-note/app/adapters/notebook.js.

The reason we need to create a new adapter is to account for the difference in case between the attribute names in our model class and the attribute names in the API. Without creating this adapter, a query parameter of {user : 1} will find no records because the attribute in the API is called User. To address this, implement the adapter class as follows:

ch6/ember-note/app/adapters/notebook.js
```
import ApplicationAdapter from './application';
import Ember from 'ember';

export default ApplicationAdapter.extend({
  query: function(store, type, query) {
    var keys = Object.keys(query);
    for(var i = 0; i < keys.length; i++) {
      var key = keys[i];
      var classifiedKey = Ember.String.classify(key);
      query[classifiedKey] = query[key];
      delete query[key];
    }
    return this._super(store, type, query);
  }
});
```

We're extending the query method to intercept queries before they get to the server. This is the method that's called on the adapter when we query using a parameter hash, as we do in the notebooks route. Our code takes the key-value pairs with the keys in camel-case, and replaces them with key-value pairs in the case expected by the API. It then passes control to the superclass method to execute the query. This enables our query to be properly recognized by the API. If you log in to the app, you should be able to add new notebooks, and see the new notebooks appear in your list, just as they did before we changed the back-end API.

## Adapt to Path Name Variations

Not only is there a means of changing the attribute names using RESTAdapter, but you can alter the path to match as well. By default, Ember Data attempts to pluralize the name of the class to arrive at the API path, so a model class called notebook will use an endpoint path of notebooks. For any number of reasons, this may not be accurate. If so, you can use the pathForType method to address this need, like this:

```
pathForType: function(type) {
  if(type === 'notebook')
    return 'poorly-named-endpoint';
}
```

As you can see, this method takes the model class name as an argument, and converts it into either a different value altogether or a somehow modified version of the name by changing the case, adding underscores, and so forth. This allows you to adapt to variations in naming conventions on the endpoint URL.

## Change the Payload Root

There's a similar method in RESTSerializer that allows you to accept a JSON payload from the server and determine the correct type based on the name of the root key. Take the following payload:

```
{
  "Notebooks" : {
    //Your payload data here!
  }
}
```

If you implement the modelNameFromPayloadKey function, you can alter the value of the root key, which allows Ember Data to properly look up the associated model class and handle the payload accordingly, like this:

```
modelNameFromPayloadKey: function(root) {
  return Ember.String.camelize(root);
}
```

This converts "Notebooks" into "notebooks" and allows Ember Data to find the appropriate model class to use for the payload.

Of course, to save back to the server, you'll need to reverse the action you took in modelNameFromPayloadKey. You can implement this in payloadKeyFromModel-Name:

```
payloadKeyFromModelName: function(modelName) {
  return Ember.String.classify(modelName);
}
```

This converts "notebooks" back to "Notebooks", which lets you save the payload back into a server with that expected format.

## Modify the Payload in Flight

We've covered most of the scenarios you're likely to see when working with a RESTful API. There is one last scenario, though. You may need to use an API that is only capable of returning composite records, such as an API response that includes child records as a child node in your JSON payload, rather than as a separate node altogether.

Let's say that a query to our notebooks API returned data in the following format:

```
{
  "notebooks": {
    "id": 1,
    "title": "notebook one",
    "description": "description one",
    "notes": [{
      "id": 1,
      "title": "note one",
      "description": "description one"
    },{
      "id": 2,
      "title": "note two",
      "description": "description two"
    }]
  }
}
```

Note that the "notes" node is nested inside the "notebooks" object. This is not the format Ember Data expects for the payload. Ember Data's expectation is that the same information have the following payload structure:

```json
{
  "notebooks": {
    "id": 1,
    "title": "notebook one",
    "description": "description one",
    "notes": [1, 2]
  },
  "notes": [{
      "id": 1,
      "title": "note one",
      "description": "description one"
    },{
      "id": 2,
      "title": "note two",
      "description": "description two"
    }]
  }
}
```

For you to make this conversion, you need to implement the extractArray method in your RESTSerializer implementation. This method allows you to perform any reformatting or cleanup on the payload. Here's an example implementation of the method:

```javascript
extractArray: function(store, type, payload) {
  //You'd perform work on the payload here, then pass on to the superclass
  return this._super(store, type, payload);
}
```

The payload method parameter is the original response from the server. Your implementation is likely to take this payload, make whatever adjustments necessary to get it into Ember Data's expected format, and then pass it on to the superclass instance of the method. Some common operations that might take place include changing the structure of the payload or deleting unneeded information, such as attributes that are not in your model. This lets you make use of even the most unconventional API responses and still take advantage of Ember Data's features.

This method is used when the payload is a response to a query containing multiple rows, such as a findMany. There's a parallel method, known as extractSingle, that fills the same role, but acts on responses that include just one record, such as a find or a save. The method signature contains one additional parameter, and looks like this:

```javascript
extractSingle: function(store, type, payload, recordId) {
  //You'd perform work on the payload here, then pass on to the superclass
  return this._super(store, type, payload, recordId);
}
```

There are many other similar methods, each of which supports a specific data operation, such as extractCreateRecord, but the most relevant ones are in essence just an alias for either extractSingle or extractArray. However, if your API requires that different operation types receive different treatment, it's worth knowing that these options are out there.

## Tie Adapters and Serializers to Your Model Class

There are two ways to go about implementing the adapter/serializer pattern in your app. We've actually used both so far. For common changes that you want to share across all REST requests, such as adding a user token, you modify the application adapter or serializer that Ember CLI creates for you, located at ember-note/app/adapters/application.js and ember-note/app/serializers/application.js. If you want to create a model-specific adapter or serializer, you run one of the following commands:

```
$ ember generate serializer mymodel
```

or

```
$ ember generate adapter mymodel
```

This creates an adapter or serializer that will be applied to requests for data of the given type. You can then implement the features we described earlier, without worrying that they will be applied unnecessarily to other model types.

Now that we've explored how to use an alternate API, let's get rid of the notebook adapter and serializer, and change our application-wide RESTAdapter back. From a command line, run the following commands:

```
$ ember destroy adapter notebook
$ ember destroy serializer notebook
```

Then modify the namespace property in the ember-note/app/adapters/application.js file as follows:

```
namespace: "api"
```

You can leave the headers in place; there's no reason they should be removed. With our brisk tour through nonconforming APIs at an end, we're ready for our next step.

## Next Steps

The RESTAdapter and RESTSerializer classes offer a lot more than we've been able to cover here. These classes provide a powerful means of using Ember Data to work with just about any API, so I encourage you to explore these further if you run into a scenario we haven't covered. We've now seen a lot of the core features of Ember and Ember Data, but there's more for us yet. Ember offers a variety of options for extending this core and for using the framework itself to link classes together to help increase the utility of the classes you create. In the next chapter, we'll extend Ember by making commonly needed utilities available throughout your app.

# CHAPTER 7

# Reusing Code in Ember

We've spent a good deal of time learning the core features of Ember. We've seen how to build web apps using these core features, and how to do so quickly, by relying on Ember's opinionated structure.

That structure does more than provide you with a means of building the core of your app. It also provides several ways of sharing code between different aspects of your system. It offers the ability to bootstrap your app by preparing any necessary objects. And it provides the ability to translate a data value from one context to another, such as a currency translation.

In this chapter, we'll look at how to use Ember and Ember CLI to layer in app-specific abstractions on top of Ember's opinionated structure so that you can apply sound design to EmberNote's logic. Let's get started by looking at the most basic level of abstraction: the utility class.

## Abstract Common Functions with Utilities

One way to share code between objects is to create a simple utility function. Ember CLI includes a blueprint for creating a utility function that can be imported into other classes. Strictly speaking, creating the utility function this way isn't a feature of the Ember core framework as much as a feature of Ember CLI. We'll discuss how Ember CLI makes this and other features possible when we explore building your app in Chapter 8, *Building, Testing, and Deploying Your Ember Apps*, on page 105.

The goal of creating a utility function is to provide a single place for logic to live that might need to be used in different, unrelated classes. I say "unrelated," because if the classes were related, we'd be better off using a mixin, as we'll see in *Share Code with Mixins*, on page 94.

Data validation is a good example of the sort of logic that might live in a utility function. There are many different reasons why you might need to validate data. You might need to validate that a string is a valid email, or phone number, or postal code. You might need to validate the length of a string, or that it's a valid date. You might need to validate that it doesn't contain certain characters. In any event, it's possible that you'll want to use such validation in several unrelated contexts, so validation is a good use case for us to start with.

For our purposes, let's say we want to validate that EmberNote's note titles have a length between 0 and 140 characters. We'll create a utility function to enforce this, and then use that function in our notes route. To begin, run the following command from your project root:

```
$ ember generate util is-valid-length
```

This command creates an empty utility function that looks like this:

```
export default function isValidLength() {
  return true;
}
```

To add our actual logic, make the following changes:

ch7/ember-note/app/utils/is-valid-length.js
```
export default function isValidLength(value, min, max) {
  return !(value.length <= min || value.length > max);
}
```

The specific implementation details of this function are less important than the form. You'll notice that the command used the dasherized text is-valid-length, whereas the function is called isValidLength. Ember CLI performs that translation when creating the function, which is captured in a file called is-valid-length.js. So now that we have a function, how do we reference it? Take a look at the following updates to our notes route:

ch7/ember-note/app/notebooks/notes/route.js
```
import Ember from 'ember';
➤ import isValidLength from 'ember-note/utils/is-valid-length';

export default Ember.Route.extend({
  model: function(params) {
    return this.store.query('note', {notebook:params.notebook_id});
  },
  actions: {
    addNote: function() {
➤     var title = this.controller.get('title');
➤     if(!isValidLength(title,0,140)) {
➤       alert('Title must be longer than 0 '
```

```
➤                    + 'characters and not more than 140.');
➤            }
➤            else {
                 this.store.query('notebook',
                   this.paramsFor('notebooks.notes').notebook_id)
                   .then(
                     (notebook) => {
                       console.log(notebook);
                       var note = this.store.createRecord('note', {
                         title : this.controller.get('title'),
                         notebook: notebook
                       });
                       console.log(note);
                       note.save().then(() => {
                         console.log('save successful');
                         this.controller.set('title',null);
                         this.refresh();
                       }, function() {
                         console.log('save failed');
                       });
                     }
                   );
➤            }
           },
           deleteNote: function(note) {
             console.log('deleting note with title ' + note.get('title'));
             note.deleteRecord();
             note.save();
           }
       }
   });
```

The import statement makes the new utility function available to the route. A few lines later, we use the function to check the length of the title before we add it, and alert the user that we're not going to save the record if the title fails validation.

It's worth noting that the new function is referred to as isValidLength in its definition in is-valid-length.js, and in both the import and invocation in the notes route. Once you define the function in the file and import it into another class, you use it as though it were defined in the class to which it was imported.

If you want to create a single function that can be imported and used throughout your app, utility functions can help. However, it's also often helpful to share a collection of such functions. One way to do this is to create a mixin, and then include it into the classes that need to use it. Let's take a look at that now.

## Share Code with Mixins

While utilities are a useful way to share one function, they don't cover every possible need. Our validation utility function could have been more useful if it were in the form of a collection of functions that could be used in many places. To do this, we can create a mixin. In Ember, a *mixin* is a collection of properties and functions that can be used in any class that depends on them. The definition of these properties and functions resides in the mixin, and is available in any class that takes advantage of the mixin.

Because a mixin can contain properties and functions, it can be used not only to abstract behavior, but to abstract state as well. When a class inherits this mixin, the properties and functions of that mixin become part of the definition of the inheriting class. A utility function can be used to perform operations on a piece of data passed to it, whereas a mixin can be used for operations and state.

Now, let's see how to create our mixin. From a command line, run the following Ember CLI command:

```
$ ember generate mixin validation-functions
```

We're going to add two validation routines to this library. We'll create one that performs the same length validation as we performed in the utility. The second will check whether a string represents a valid email address.

Update the newly created mixin class to the following:

ch7/ember-note/app/mixins/validation-functions.js
```
import Ember from 'ember';

export default Ember.Mixin.create({
  isValidLength: function(value, min, max) {
    return !(value === undefined
      || value.length <= min || value.length > max);
  },
  isValidEmail: function(value) {
    var pattern = /^\w+([\.-]?\w+)*@\w+([\.-]?\w+)*(\.\w{2,3})+$/;
    return value.match(pattern);
  }
});
```

This mixin consists of two functions: isValidLength and isValidEmail. The isValidLength function is nearly identical to the version of this function defined in ember-note/app/utils/is-valid-length.js. The only substantial difference is that the version of it in the mixin is a property of the Mixin object, whereas the utility version stands on its own.

## Regular Expressions

The isValidEmail function uses a *regular expression* to determine if the passed-in string represents an email address. Regular expressions are a means of capturing the expected format of a piece of data, called a *pattern*, and then using that to verify whether an actual piece of data follows that format.

As you can see from the pattern variable in isValidEmail, a regular expression often takes the form of a complex-looking string of characters, and these patterns can often grow to an unexpectedly large size. In our earlier example, the email validation is only 48 characters, but it doesn't allow for new top-level domains, such as .museum, to be used. There are alternative patterns for validating an email address that run into the thousands of characters. Given this complexity, you could argue that you're better off just trying to send a confirmation email to make sure the address is valid.

The point is, regular expressions are extremely useful but getting them right is challenging. If you need to use regular expressions, be prepared to write fairly robust test cases, and then expand on them as issues arise. We could probably spend an entire book on regular expressions, so my advice is to use them judiciously.

A few minor changes are required to update the notes route to use the mixin. Make the following changes to the route:

```
// Replace the import of 'is-valid-length'
import ValidationFunctions from 'ember-note/mixins/validation-functions';
// ...
// Change the class declaration of the route
export default Ember.Route.extend(ValidationFunctions,{
// ...
// Change how the function is referenced
if(!this.isValidLength(title,0,140)) {
// ...
```

The first change is to simply replace the import of is-valid-length with an import of the mixin. Once we've done that, we add the name of the mixin to the declaration of the route, which takes the properties and functions of the mixin and makes them part of the route.

Once the mixin is folded into the route class, we access the function we want by calling this.isValidLength. Because the mixin is made a part of the route's object definition, we use this to gain access to it. The difference between using this form and the utility class is that the mixin can offer more sophisticated features because it's able to provide its own state that can be accessed by the object that uses it.

Now let's see how we can use the isValidEmail function to alter the registration route to require an email address as the username. Change the register route as follows:

```
ch7/ember-note/app/register/route.js
import Ember from 'ember';
import ValidationFunctions from 'ember-note/mixins/validation-functions';

export default Ember.Route.extend(ValidationFunctions,{
  actions : {
    addNew : function() {
      var name = this.controller.get('name');
      if(this.isValidEmail(name)) {
        var user = this.store.createRecord('user', {
          name : name
        });
        user.save().then(() => {
          console.log('save successful');
          this.controller.set('message',
            'A new user with the name "' + name + '" was added!');
          this.controller.set('name',null);
        }, function() {
          console.log('save failed');
        });
      }
      else {
        alert('Invalid email address.');
      }
    }
  }
});
```

The changes to the register route are very similar to the changes we made to the notes route. First, we need to import the ValidationFunctions mixin. Then we refer to it when we extend the Ember.Route, so the mixin will be made part of the new route. Then, as we did in the notes route, we call it using this.isValidEmail, and proceed with the addNew action if the validation passes. We display a message to the user if not.

While we've defined isValidLength and isValidEmail as functions, these properties could have just as easily held a value. If they had, the including class (in this case, the notes route) would have access to them, just like it has access to the functions.

Mixins are a great way to share code, but Ember has even more to offer. Sometimes, you'll want to share access to state or to services. Ember has a way to do that called *dependency injection,* which you'll learn about next.

## Ember Addon: Validation

Our example validation class is great for illustrating the ideas behind a mixin, but it's nowhere near mature. For a much more complete example of how to use a mixin to perform validation, check out the ember-validations addon, published by Dockyard. Dockyard is a major part of the team behind Ember and Ember CLI.

To make use of ember-validations within your app, you install it by running the following command from your project root:

```
$ ember install ember-validations
```

This addon makes use of the ability to add properties to a class using a mixin. To add validation rules to a class, you initialize a property called validations. This property holds a JSON object, consisting of name-value pairs. The names are the properties on the class that you wish to validate, and the values are a JSON object containing the rules you want to apply to that property. For example, take a look at this code from the ember-validations documentation:

```
export default Ember.Object.extend(EmberValidations.Mixin,{
  validations: {
    firstName: {
      presence: true,
      length: { minimum: 5 }
    },
    age: {
      numericality: true
    }
  }
});
```

Adding the validations property to an object, like you're doing here, activates this addon for the object. The validation rules you want to apply are then contained in the validations property. The containing object will then be validated to ensure that the firstName property is populated and has a minimum length of 5. The age is validated to ensure that it's a number. There are several other validation options, such as format, which is used to test a regular expression, and inclusion, which provides a list of values that the property must match.

Each validation can provide a custom message, and the mixin provides a property called isValid to let you know whether or not the object contains valid data. This property will be updated each time a property is set. The messages can be accessed by referencing a property called errors.propertyName on the object. These messages can then be displayed to users to give them a chance to update the property value.

For the complete documentation, take a look at github.com/dockyard/ember-validations.

# Share Services with Dependency Injection

The features we've covered so far help you implement a sound design by creating reusable classes and sharing them across objects. Mixins and utilities are great for abstracting behavior, but for more complex abstractions, you'll want to create a service and use dependency injection to sprinkle it throughout your app.

"Service" can be interpreted to mean different things, so let's start by defining what we mean by a service. A *service* is a self-contained unit of functionality. It provides unrelated objects access to its functionality in a loosely coupled way. Ember relies on a few services out of the box. For instance, the application's instance of Ember.Router is a good example of a service: it manages the URL hierarchy in a single place and provides access to that hierarchy to other objects, particularly instances of Ember.Route, via the this.router property. Another example is Ember Data, which is a service that's made available throughout the app for data access via the store property.

For a service to be made available in a loosely coupled way, Ember needs to provide a way to get that service to the objects that need it. It does this via dependency injection. *Dependency injection* is the means of providing a service to the object that relies on it. The goal of dependency injection is to provide this service in such a way as for the client to have minimal knowledge of the service.

In the dependency injection pattern, the service (that is, the dependency) is instantiated external to the client, and later injected into the client. Ember, therefore, needs a place to both instantiate the dependency and inject it into the client. Let's take a look at initializers.

## Using Initializers

To make dependency injection work, Ember must do some work during the initial load of the app into the browser. It's important that this take place very early in the app's life cycle, since the type of services that typically use dependency injection are often used in many different places throughout the app. To accomplish this, you can use the Ember.Application.initializer function.

This function accepts an object, whose only requirement is that it define a function called initialize. This function is used to perform whatever work you need done at startup time.

We've already used initializers in *Creating and Injecting a User Session*, on page 78, but we're going to create a second one now to centralize logging behavior. Run the following command:

```
$ ember generate initializer logger
```

When we run this command, Ember CLI creates an empty initializer stub:

```
export function initialize(/* container, application */) {
  // application.inject('route', 'foo', 'service:foo');
}

export default {
  name: 'logger',
  initialize: initialize
};
```

When your user first opens your app, the initialize function will be run for each initializer you've created. Of course, you may need to control the order in which they run. For that, Ember follows the order you define. If you notice, the initializer includes a name attribute.

You may also use an attribute called before and one called after. Each attribute accepts either a string or an array of strings. The before and after attributes use the name property of other initializers to determine an execution order. If an array is passed to these attributes, then each of the initializers in the array is considered.

Initializers can be used for any app-wide work you need to perform, but one of their chief use cases is for dependency injection. Let's take a look at that now.

## Injecting Classes

When you're designing your app with a service-based approach in mind, you create objects that are made to be reused throughout the app. We've seen a few approaches to distributing such objects, but my favorite is to use dependency injection.

To use dependency injection in Ember, you generally perform two steps. First, you register the service with the container; then you inject it into any class factory that you want to have access to it.

The following code demonstrates how to implement these steps to inject our new logger initializer:

```
ch7/ember-note/app/initializers/logger.js
import Ember from 'ember';

export function initialize(registry, application) {
  var logger = Ember.Object.extend({
    log: function(message) {
      console.log(message);
    }
  });
  application.register('logger:main', logger);
  application.inject('route','logger','logger:main');
}

export default {
  name: 'logger',
  initialize: initialize
};
```

The first thing we do is to create our logger implementation. It's an extension of Ember.Object, and has a simple one-parameter wrapper around the JavaScript console object.

Next, we register this new class using the register method of the Ember.Application object passed in to the initialize function. The register method accepts up to three parameters: the name of the object registered (logger:main), the factory (the logger variable that points to our new class), and an options hash.

The options hash can contain two properties: instantiate and singleton. By default, the factory's create method will be called unless an options hash is passed with a value of false. If singleton is false, then multiple instances of this object could be created when the object is looked up; otherwise the same instance is returned from each lookup.

The inject method is what takes this newly registered factory and makes it available throughout the app. The inject method takes three parameters. The first is the name of the factory into which your new factory is injected. In our case, we're injecting our new logger into each route implementation by passing the route factory into inject. You can inject into specific implementations by identifying them by name (for example, route:notebooks). The second parameter is the name of the property that will receive the instance of the new factory. This property is how you reference the injected service from the client class. And last, the third parameter is the injection name of the factory you want to inject, which should match the name it was registered under (for example, logger:main).

Once the injection is completed during the app's initialization process, it's available under the assigned property name in each instance into which it was injected. The following code demonstrates the use of an injected service from a class:

```
ch7/ember-note/app/notebooks/route.js
import Ember from 'ember';

export default Ember.Route.extend({
  model: function(params) {
    return this.store.query('notebook',{user: params.user_id});
  },
  actions: {
    addNotebook: function() {
      var notebook = this.store.createRecord('notebook', {
        title: this.controller.get('title'),
        user: this.session.get('user')
      });
      notebook.save().then(() => {
        this.logger.log('save successful');
        this.controller.set('title',null);
        this.refresh();
      }, () => {
        this.logger.log('save failed');
      });
    }
  }

});
```

With the logging class registered and injected in the initializer, a property called logger is available in all of your app's instances of Ember.Route. The figure on page 102 illustrates how these pieces fit together:

The Ember Data framework uses dependency injection to good effect. When you reference the store property in your route implementations, it's because that property was set via an injection initializer that Ember Data set up.

There's an alternative to globally injecting a service into an object factory. If you want to use a service in a more limited subset of objects, you can use a different API to obtain the service from within only the class you want impacted.

Let's say you have a service called foo that you want to use from a single route. You can create a property that accesses the service like this:

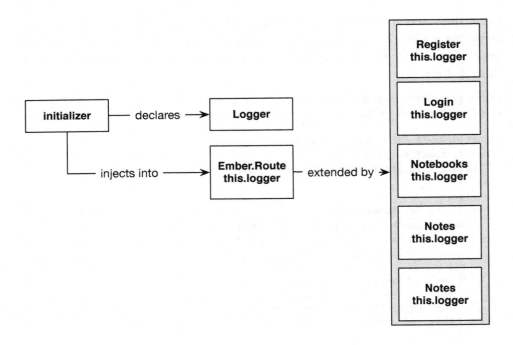

```
import Ember from 'ember';

export default Ember.Route.extend({
  fooService: Ember.inject.service('foo'),
  model: function(params) {
    return this.fooService.mumblyFoo(params.foobar);
  }
});
```

Assuming that you have registered a service called foo in your initializer, you can access it using Ember.inject.service. The one distinction is that in the initializer, rather than register the foo service under foo:main, you need to register it under service:foo, or the container may have trouble looking it up.

Utilities, mixins, and dependency injection are three helpful ways of making your code more modular, and I encourage you to consider using any of these in the appropriate context. Before moving on to our next chapter, we have one more brief foray into abstraction. In the next section, I'll discuss how to use app-specific data types in your models with Ember Data transforms.

## Use Transforms to Tweak Data

If you're using Ember Data to access a legacy API, or even to use data from an upstream data source, you may need to perform some transformation on a data value before using it in your app. For this use case, Ember Data includes the DS.Transform class. A DS.Transform encapsulates the logic needed to take data from one form into the desired form.

Ember Data comes with a few built-in DS.Transform implementations: DS.BooleanTransform, DS.DateTransform, and DS.NumberTransform. Each of these is responsible for taking data from a non-canonical form and translating it into the expected form. For example, DS.BooleanTransform is able to take raw JSON with a value of "true" or 1 and transform it into a Boolean true.

Let's see how this could work for another transformation. Imagine a use case where your app accessed financial transaction data that originated from an upstream data source. Complicating matters is the fact that these transactions are stored in US dollars. The app wants to display all such data points in the user's native currency. A DS.Transform can help.

To get started, you execute the following Ember CLI command:

```
$ ember generate transform native-currency
```

This command generates an empty transform stub. The following example illustrates how the transform would be built:

```
import DS from 'ember-data';

export default DS.Transform.extend({
  deserialize: function(serialized) {

    // Perform your currency translation here
    var amountInNative =
      this.currencyTranslator.translateToNative(serialized);
    return amountInNative;
  },

  serialize: function(deserialized) {

    // Translate from native to USD
    var amountInUSD = this.currencyTranslator.translateToUSD(deserialized);
    return amountInUSD;
  }
});
```

In this example, we assume that a user-specific translation object has been created and injected into the transform. This will allow us to compute translations that use the user's currency translation rate. The transform itself is simply responsible for stepping in when a model requests information in the native currency. An example model class that needs to use the transform would look like this:

```
import DS from "ember-data";

export default DS.Model.extend({
  toAccount: DS.attr('string'),
  fromAccount: DS.attr('string'),
  amount: DS.attr('native-currency') // Amount in native currency
});
```

The same data could be represented without using the transform like this:

```
import DS from "ember-data";

export default DS.Model.extend({
  toAccount: DS.attr('string'),
  fromAccount: DS.attr('string'),
  amount: DS.attr('number') // Amount in USD as kept in the data store
});
```

The transform works both to deserialize the data (that is, translate from its stored format to its displayed format), and to serialize the data. This means that you can display in your chosen format, but when it's time to save, the serialize function steps in and converts the data back into the appropriate format, to remain consistent with the database's expectations.

## Next Steps

We spent the majority of our time together learning how to build Ember apps. Building an app is great, but you want to get it in front of people, right? In the next two chapters you'll learn a bit more about Ember CLI, which helps greatly in the deploy and release process. Next up, you'll learn how to use it to manage dependencies and build a deployable artifact from your Ember code. As part of that process, we'll also look at how to use the test hooks Ember CLI provides so that we can be confident in our code.

# CHAPTER 8

# Building, Testing, and Deploying Your Ember Apps

We've done a great deal of work so far building our app's features. But there's another important area we need to address before we're done. We need to spend some time thinking about how to make our app ready for production.

Ember CLI does a lot of this work for us, but it will help you as a developer to understand a little of what's going on behind the scenes. To begin, we'll take a look at how Ember CLI prepares a usable version of your application from the code you create. Then, we'll spend the majority of this chapter discussing how Ember CLI helps you test your app. Last, we'll take a look at how Ember CLI helps you deploy your application.

Let's get started by looking at how Ember CLI builds your application code and keeps it ready for you to run at a moment's notice.

## Build Your App

If you've worked in JavaScript (or any other software development tool) for long you're probably familiar with one common roadblock: the build system. Like with languages, everybody has a different opinion about what is the best build system for a given language. Closely related to this choice is your choice of dependency management. Choosing a build and dependency management tool is one challenge; configuring the chosen toolset is another. Thankfully, Ember CLI elegantly solves this issue for you.

### Getting Your Dependencies

When you first install Ember CLI, it includes the most current version of Ember. As part of the Ember 2.x release cycle, the Ember core and Ember

CLI will synchronize release schedules. As such, if you want to upgrade Ember CLI, Ember should follow. You can upgrade Ember CLI by running the following commands as an administrative user in your project directory:

```
$ npm uninstall -g ember-cli
$ npm cache clean
$ bower cache clean
$ npm install -g ember-cli
$ npm install ember-cli --save-dev
$ rm -rf node_modules bower_components dist tmp
$ npm install
$ bower install
$ ember init
```

The first three commands remove the current version of Ember CLI from the npm package management system and clear out related files from both the npm and Bower caches. Next, the latest Ember CLI is installed and made available globally (as defined by the -g flag), and also installed into your project's package.json file (where we use the --save-dev flag).

Then, to be safe, we remove the four directories in our app that contain dependencies and built versions of our apps. The next two commands reinstall all of the dependencies listed in package.json and bower.json into your local components directories. Lastly, ember init reruns all of the Ember CLI blueprints against your current codebase to look for changes. You've used these blueprints every time you've run ember generate, and because the blueprints can change, it's good to reapply them. The command gives you the chance to approve each diff listed, so you're aware of what's changed by this command. Be careful here—some of the changes might remove code you want to keep, depending on what's changed in Ember CLI, so it's best to be cautious. You're using a good version control system, right?

There may be times when you want to simply update one of your dependencies without updating Ember CLI. Because Ember CLI relies on Bower, you can simply install an updated dependency by running the following:

```
$ bower install my-dependency --save
```

This will update your bower.json so the dependency becomes part of your project.

## Running Your App Locally

As you're coding or changing dependencies, Ember CLI keeps the local deployment up to date, assuming you have a running instance launched via the ember serve command. Ember CLI builds a locally deployable version of the app, including your mock server, and starts this app.

As we've seen throughout the book, when you run the ember serve command, it launches the watchman service. When watchman detects a change in one of your app's files, it triggers a rebuild of the app. Further, when you browse to the app, the locally deployed version contains a WebSockets client that monitors for changes and reloads your app in the browser if necessary. This is pretty handy, particularly when you're coding fast and want to see changes just as fast. One other thing you'll want to do when you're coding fast is to write test cases. We'll see how to do that now.

# Test and Debug Your App

I've been keeping a little secret this whole time. Ember CLI doesn't just generate your classes for you when you run an ember generate. It generates test harnesses for you as well. In fact, they are complete enough to be runnable (though they don't offer much in the way of coverage). If you're among those who have had a hard time in the past with applying good testing practices to your JavaScript client code, your last excuse just fell away.

## Test Execution

Let's start by reviewing the current test results for the tests that Ember CLI has created as we work. Open a command prompt, navigate to the root of the EmberNote project, and run the following:

```
$ ember test
```

When you run this command, you should see your console filling with output. Ember CLI will first build your app, then run the tests it has been generating throughout your work.

There's a second way to view your tests. From the same command prompt, press Ctrl-C, which halts the paused output of ember test. It should report a few failing tests, which we'll get to in a moment. First, run ember serve from the command line. Then, point your browser at localhost:4200/tests.

In your browser, you'll see the results of your tests displayed. Scroll through the results and you should see the failing tests. Before we fix a few of these failing tests (and yes, the tests do require some tweaking), let's talk a little bit about the tooling Ember CLI uses to accomplish test execution.

When you run the ember test command from the command line, Ember CLI spins up a PhantomJS instance. PhantomJS is a headless web browser (a browser with no user interface), written entirely in JavaScript. By using PhantomJS, you're able to execute your tests as part of a continuous integration process. *Continuous integration* is the practice of regularly compiling your software with an automated process on a dedicated build machine. Using continuous integration, you can check if errors have been introduced by new changes. If you adopt continuous integration, your tests should be run during the build process. Using PhantomJS allows your testing to occur without requiring a traditional browser be installed on the continuous integration machine.

When you run the tests by visiting localhost:4200/tests, you're actually using an Ember application that Ember CLI builds as you update your app. This app is built to run your tests and display the results to you. It runs every test, and offers you a few options to determine which test results you want to see.

Both of these methods for reviewing your test results are useful, and both have a place in your development plans. Throughout the rest of the chapter, we'll rely on the test app viewable at localhost:4200, as it offers a slightly better user experience.

With a way to look at our test results, let's start by writing the more foundational of the tests we're going to write: unit tests.

## Writing Unit Tests

One benefit of being able to use a module-based approach to JavaScript is that we can think in a modular fashion about our tests as well. Ember CLI creates one test module for each app module we create. Let's see one of those now. When you created the note model class, Ember CLI created a test in a file called note-test.js, in the ember-note/tests/unit directory. The generated file looks like this:

```
ch8/ember-note/tests/unit/models/notebook-test.js
import {
  moduleForModel,
  test
} from 'ember-qunit';

moduleForModel('notebook', 'Unit | Model | notebook', {
  // Specify the other units that are required for this test.
  needs: [];
});

test('it exists', function(assert) {
  var model = this.subject();
  // var store = this.store();
  assert.ok(!!model);
});
```

The import block pulls in the moduleForModel and test functions from ember-qunit. These functions are used in the test class to load the class we want to test and then execute a test against it, respectively.

---

**QUnit, ember-test-helpers, and ember-qunit**

To test using the ember test command or via the browser, you'll primarily rely on three test frameworks: QUnit (qunitjs.com), ember-test-helpers (github.com/switchfly/ember-test-helpers), and ember-qunit (github.com/rwjblue/ember-qunit).

Each of these plays a role in providing some of the code you write for test cases. QUnit is a generic JavaScript testing framework written originally for jQuery; ember-test-helpers is an Ember-specific set of test harnesses that requires a specific test framework, such as QUnit, to function; and ember-qunit glues the two of these together.

---

### Test Case Dependencies

This generated unit test will confirm the most fundamental behavior: that an instance of the note model class can be created. And right now, this test is a failing test. If you look at the test result, you should see a message that reads something like "No model was found for notebook." Why is it reporting that it can't find the notebook model? Because the note model class contains a belongsTo reference to notebook. Let's fix that. Change the needs array of your test case to look like this:

ch8/ember-note/tests/unit/models/notebook-test.js
```
needs: [
  'model:user',
  'model:note'
];
```

Once you make that change, the failing notebook model tests should pass. Rerun your tests via the browser to confirm. If you want a clean set of tests, you can also make similar changes to the note tests to get them to pass as well.

You'll also want to make a few changes to the application serializer's test case for it to pass. Update the moduleForModel code as follows:

ch8/ember-note/tests/unit/serializers/application-test.js
```
moduleForModel('user', 'Unit | Serializer | application', {
  // Specify the other units that are required for this test.
  needs: ['model:user']
});
```

This change updates the serializer test to rely on one of our model classes, the user model. The Ember CLI test blueprint for the serializer test class looks for a model called application, which doesn't exist in our app. Changing to a class that does exist allows this test to pass.

With these changes, we've updated most of the tests to use the proper dependencies. You may note that the edit-note test is failing right now. Leave that one as is. We'll come to it soon. First, let's look at how to write unit tests for our models.

### Unit Testing Your Models

Under many circumstances, you may not need to write test cases for your model classes. If your model classes rely solely on framework-defined behavior, as ours do, you won't even need to write test cases. But let's complicate things for ourselves a bit, and add a function to our notebook model that counts the number of notes associated to the notebook instance. Update your notebook model to look like this:

ch8/ember-note/app/models/notebook.js
```
import DS from 'ember-data';

export default DS.Model.extend({
  title : DS.attr('string'),
  user : DS.belongsTo('user'),
  notes : DS.hasMany('note'),
  noteCount: function() {
    return this.get('notes.length');
  }
});
```

The noteCount function gets a copy of the notes attribute, which points to the array of associated notes, and returns the length of that array. That's what it's meant to do. Now, let's write a test that confirms this. Update your notebook-test.js file to look like this:

ch8/ember-note/tests/unit/models/notebook-test.js
```
import {
  moduleForModel,
  test
} from 'ember-qunit';
import Ember from 'ember';

moduleForModel('notebook', 'Unit | Model | notebook', {
  // Specify the other units that are required for this test.
  needs: [
    'model:user',
    'model:note'
```

```
  ];
});

test('it exists', function(assert) {
  var model = this.subject();
  // var store = this.store();
  assert.ok(!!model);
});

test('it counts notes', function(assert) {
  var notebook = this.subject({ title: 'my notebook' });
  var note;
  var noteCount = Math.floor(Math.random() * (10 - 1) + 1);

  Ember.run(() => {
    for(var i = 0; i < noteCount; i++) {
      note = this.store().createRecord('note');
      notebook.get('notes').addObject(note);
    }
  });

  assert.equal(notebook.noteCount(),noteCount);
});
```

First, we'll need to modify our imports to include the Ember class. (We'll see why shortly.) Having done so we add a new test to the end of the file with the description of "it counts notes." These descriptions are used by the test runner to tell you which test it's running.

Next, we'll do some setup work. The call to this.subject creates an instance of the notebook class that we're going to use to test. We'll then initialize a variable called note that we'll populate with note instances. And we'll create a random number between 1 and 10, to test that the right number of note instances are added to the notebook.

Here's where we'll use the instance of Ember imported earlier. Because the work we're about to do runs asynchronously and has side effects, the test runner requires that we do this work inside our own run loop. Within that run loop, we'll use the random number from earlier to generate the expected number of note instances, and then add them to the notebook.

At this point you might be unsure as to when to use Ember.run and when not to. Rest assured, the test runner is very clear about why a given test won't run and will provide an error message indicating that your code requires Ember.run. Other than that, the details about Ember.run are mostly relevant if you're working *on* Ember instead of *with* Ember.

With that setup work performed, we'll run the actual test by asserting that the noteCount method returns the expected number of records: the random number declared earlier. Our test should pass, and we can sleep a bit better knowing that we have one fewer method to worry about.

---

**Random Number Generation**

 Random number generation is a risky area if security is involved. The Math.random function we used earlier is fine for the way we used it, but you shouldn't use it for anything that requires security, such as generating a random value for two-factor authentication or a captcha, because the output of Math.random is not truly random. In these cases, you're better off using the RandomSource.getRandomValues() function, as documented on the Mozilla Developer Network at developer.mozilla.org/en-US/docs/Web/API/RandomSource/getRandomValues.

---

Now, let's take a look at how to unit test our components.

## Unit Testing Your Components

As I mentioned earlier, we want to focus our unit testing on pieces of code that are not already tested by the framework. Another criterion to use to determine whether a class is ripe for unit testing is whether it relies on externalities, such as the Ember Data store, that are difficult to mock. Our edit-note component currently has two actions: saveNote and closeNote. Let's take a quick look back at the class:

```
ch8/ember-note/app/components/edit-note/component.js
import Ember from 'ember';

export default Ember.Component.extend({
  actions: {
    saveNote: function() {
      this.get('note').save();
    },
    closeNote: function() {
      this.sendAction('close');
    }
  }
});
```

Behind the scenes, saveNote is calling out to the store to save data, so this method will need to rely on an acceptance test. We can still unit test it, though, to some degree. A better candidate for a unit test is the closeNote action, which simply refers the action to a class that's passed to the component. This class can be easily mocked.

Let's make a small tweak to the edit-note template. For each of the buttons, add an id parameter, like this:

```
ch8/ember-note/app/components/edit-note/template.hbs
<div>
  {{input value=note.title}}
  <button id="save" {{action "saveNote"}}>save</button>
  <button id="close" {{action "closeNote"}}>close</button>
</div>
<div>
  {{textarea rows=10 cols=60 value=note.body}}
</div>
<div>
  {{markdown-to-html markdown=note.body}}
</div>
<div>
  {{yield}}
</div>
```

You'll see why we added these attributes in a moment. Let's take a look at how we would write tests for the component by reviewing the component test class, with a few new tests added:

```
ch8/ember-note/tests/integration/components/edit-note/component-test.js
import {
  moduleForComponent,
  test
} from 'ember-qunit';

import Ember from 'ember';

moduleForComponent('edit-note', {
  // Specify the other units that are required for this test
  needs: ['component:markdown-to-html']
});

test('it renders', function(assert) {
  assert.expect(2);

  // Creates the component instance
  var component = this.subject();
  assert.equal(component._state, 'preRender');

  // Renders the component to the page
  this.render();
  assert.equal(component._state, 'inDOM');
});

test('it saves', function(assert) {
  var component = this.subject();
```

```
  this.render();
  var saveTarget = {
    save: function() {
      assert.ok(true,'saved the note');
    }
  };
  Ember.run(() => {
    component.set('note',saveTarget);
  });
  this.$().find('#save').click();
});

test('it closes', function(assert) {
  var component = this.subject();
  this.render();
  var closeTarget = {
    closeAction: function() {
      assert.ok(true,'closed the window');
    }
  };
  component.set('close','closeAction');
  component.set('targetObject',closeTarget);
  this.$().find('#close').click();
});
```

We've added the Ember class again because we'll need to use the run loop in one of our tests. In moduleForComponent, we added a dependency on the markdown-to-html addon so that the test framework knows to use this class in rendering the edit-note component.

The "it renders" test is Ember CLI test boilerplate for a component. We haven't altered it. This tests whether the component is set up and rendered as expected by the test container.

Our first test is the "it saves" test. As we've seen in our model test, the first task of this test is to create an instance of the object to be tested. We then render it to the "screen." Once that setup work is performed, we create a mock object to act in the role of a note model. This mock object needs to contain just one method: the save method. In this case, because we want to verify that this method is properly called by the component, we put our assertion in this method. If the method is called, the referenced message will be printed and the test will pass.

With our mock object created, we use the Ember.run method to wrap the component.set action, since the re-render caused by the model change will happen asynchronously and have side effects (namely, updating the DOM). Then, we force a click action on the named button object. This causes the component's saveNote action to fire, which is supposed to run the save function on the mock object. Because it does, our test passes.

The "it closes" test is rather similar. We get a component instance, render it, and create a mock object that contains the method we want to run. The significant difference is in how we link up the test objects.

Because our assignments have no side effects, we're able to run them without using the Ember.run loop. We set the value of the template's close parameter to the function we plan to run from the mock object, and set targetObject to our mock object. In a running app, the route that includes this component plays the role of the target. Because the closeNote action uses sendAction to do its work, the click in our test calls out to our closeAction in the mock object, and our test passes.

Of course, your components may have different custom code that requires testing. These two examples are good for some component-specific features, such as confirming that the component properly handles the passed-in model and confirming that it properly handles referred actions.

As I mentioned earlier, unit tests are best for testing features that don't have a lot of interaction with app-wide code or require complicated mocks. The primary type of object we haven't covered yet is routes. The reason we won't spend much time on unit testing routes is that they have a great deal of interaction with app-wide code. As such, they are much better candidates for acceptance testing than unit testing.

You're likely to write a number of unit tests that address object types besides models or components. While the details will vary by implementation, the ideas will be the same. Start with the test blueprint that Ember CLI creates and add to it as needed to confirm the behavior you've added to your classes as you go.

Unit testing is great for working at a low level, but at some point you'll want to be able to test a more complete cycle of behavior. For that, you have acceptance testing, which we'll take a look at next.

## Writing Acceptance Tests

Acceptance tests are used to test a sequence of events through the application to ensure that the correct result is achieved. It's a good way to work your way through a set of screens and give them a spin. Due to this, they require a bit more work on our end to get up and running, but they are a powerful way to confirm functionality and even detect regressions as you're adding code.

In our case, we'll work through a relatively small example. We're going to write an acceptance test to confirm that our register route is properly registering valid users. We'll create a test that starts the app, navigates to the register route, fills out the field and clicks the button, and then confirms that the correct message is displayed.

Because acceptance tests are so tailored to your app, they aren't generated by Ember CLI as you go along. To start the acceptance test, run the following command from your project root:

```
$ ember generate acceptance-test register
```

This command creates a boilerplate acceptance test for the route named in the command. Let's go ahead and modify it to look like the following:

ch8/ember-note/tests/acceptance/register-test.js
```
import Ember from 'ember';
import { module, test } from 'qunit';
import startApp from 'ember-note/tests/helpers/start-app';

var application;

module('Acceptance | register', {
  beforeEach: function() {
    application = startApp();
  },

  afterEach: function() {
    Ember.run(application, 'destroy');
  }
});

test('visiting /register', function(assert) {
  visit('/register');

  fillIn('#name','test@pragprog.com');
  click('#register');

  andThen(function() {
    assert.equal(find('#message').text().trim(),
      'A new user with the name "test@pragprog.com" was added!');
    assert.equal(currentURL(), '/register');
  });
});
```

We're going to rely on some id attributes again, so update the register template to look like this (with id attributes for the input, button, and message div):

```
ch8/ember-note/app/register/template.hbs
<div class="col-md-12">
  Register new user: {{input id='name' value=name}}
  <button id='register' {{action 'addNew'}}>Add</button>
</div>
<div id='message' class="col-md-12">
  {{message}}
</div>
```

This test looks a little different from the unit tests we've been writing. The first difference you'll notice is that we're actually creating an instance of the full application. We'll need to do this in order to test cross-cutting features. beforeEach creates our app instance, and afterEach destroys it.

Next, the first step in our actual test is to navigate to the chosen URL. Because we want to test that we can register successfully, we populate the name text field with our desired value, and then click the register button.

Once we've clicked the button, we wrap our assertions in the andThen function, so we respect any asynchronous functions that came before. When it's ready, the andThen block verifies that the correct message is displayed, and that we haven't been redirected to another route.

Acceptance tests and unit tests offer a good deal of coverage of your code. By relying on these as needed, you can do a lot to ensure that you capture bugs and don't introduce new ones when code changes. Still, bugs will eventually get through, and that's when you'll need the Ember Inspector.

## Debugging with the Ember Inspector

Try as we might, sometimes writing good tests just isn't enough. There will be times when you'll need to debug your application, and you won't be able to do it just by looking at code running in your tests. Luckily, Ember has a special solution for you to use in just this case: the Ember Inspector.

The Ember Inspector is a browser addon that helps you to debug your Ember app by giving you deep access into the app's object model using Ember nomenclature. It's available by searching for "ember inspector" in the Chrome Web Store[1] or via the Firefox Addons site.[2] Go ahead and install into one of those browsers, then reload the app.

Once you've installed the Ember Inspector, you can access it by opening the developer tools in your browser. The Inspector allows you to visualize the

---

1.  chrome.google.com/webstore/search
2.  addons.mozilla.org

state of each of your Ember objects. If you set a breakpoint in your code, the Inspector will display the state of your application at that breakpoint.

If you're curious, give the Inspector a try. A good place to begin is by loading the Inspector while sitting on the login page. Before you log in, move over to the Data tab in the Inspector. Once you log in, you should see the user and notebook model types begin to reflect that you've loaded data.

One other useful feature is the Deprecations tab. This tab helps you to identify outdated use of the Ember framework. If you have existing code that you're in the process of migrating to Ember 2, this can be helpful in that migration effort.

Lastly, the Container tab of the Inspector, which is shown in the following figure, shows you each and every object you've created and some that Ember created for you. This can be useful in observing the data in objects like injected services, such as our session object.

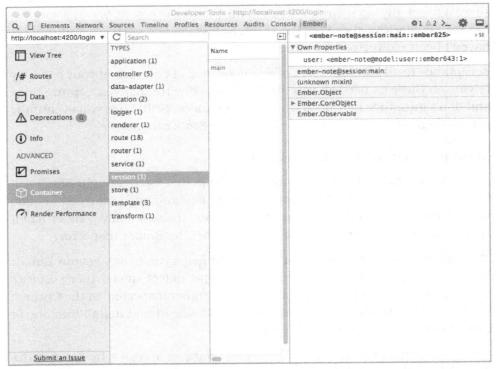

With a deep, browser-based object model such as Ember's, you need rich debugging tools. As with many things, Ember has solved this problem in a useful and intuitive way. Before we wrap up this chapter, let's take a look at how you can create deployable Ember artifacts using Ember CLI.

## Deploy Your App

It's been a long road to get here, but at last you're ready to deploy your app. Maybe you're putting it onto a development server, maybe to production. In either case, you're going to put it out somewhere for the world to see.

Ember CLI ships with a command to create a deployable artifact set for your application. From a command prompt, run the following:

```
$ ember build
```

This runs the development version of your build by default. The resulting artifacts will be located in the ember-note/dist directory. These include a JavaScript file and stylesheet named for the app (ember-note.js and ember-note.css), and a file containing the dependencies for those files (vendor.js and vendor.css). A number of other files are also included to support the test application, as well as crossdomain.xml and robots.txt, and of course your root index.html.

If you want to deploy to production, though, you have different needs. If you take a look at the ember-note.js, ember-note.css, vendor.js, and vendor.css files, they are relatively easy to read and debug. But they are also bloated, and always named the same thing, which means they are slow to load and cached by the browser.

To deploy a production-grade build, you'll want to run the ember build command with the --environment production flag set. This generates versions of those files that are minified where appropriate, and uniquely named so as not to be cached. The test files are excluded. These artifacts can be placed on your chosen high-performing web server, and your app is ready for the world to see. Another often difficult problem solved by Ember.

## Next Steps

We've seen how Ember CLI helps you to build, test, debug, and deploy your app. But we're not quite done yet. Along the way to delivering your killer app with Ember, you've likely used some addons, and possibly created some code you think others would find useful. In the last chapter, we'll take a closer look at how to find and install addons into your app. We'll also see how to publish an addon, either to a private repository for sharing between your own apps, or to a public repository for sharing with the world.

# CHAPTER 9

# Building and Using Ember Addons

Throughout the book we've seen a number of examples of Ember addons. An *addon* is a modular piece of code to be used within an Ember application. Addons can make your job easier, and the community spirit around creating and sharing Ember addons is one of the most enticing reasons to use Ember.

In this chapter, we take a closer look at the life cycle of an addon. First, you'll learn how to install an addon, which we've touched on already in *Nesting Components*, on page 55, but will cover in a bit more detail here. Next, we'll talk about how to develop your own addon, and then make it available to other Ember developers so that you can share something cool that you've made. There's nothing more satisfying than giving back to the community (unless it's bragging rights from making something that's widely used).

To begin, let's review how to get an addon installed into our app.

## Install an Ember Addon

Ember addons aren't technically a feature of Ember, but rather a feature of Ember CLI. This distinction is important because if you decide to use Ember without Ember CLI, this chapter will not apply. If you want addons, you need Ember CLI.

This becomes apparent when you look at how to obtain an Ember addon. We've already done this once in *Nesting Components*, on page 55, when we pulled in the ember-cli-showdown addon to format our text using Markdown. In order to get that addon, we ran the following command from the ember-note root:

```
$ ember install ember-cli-showdown
```

When you run this command, Ember CLI searches the npm database for the requested addon and installs it into your project in the node_modules directory.

You can then use the addon just as you would any other code that is part of your application. The addon's documentation, generally contained in its README.md file, should describe how to use the addon in your app.

There are a few different ways of discovering addons to use. My preference, which I used most in writing this book, is via Ember Observer.[1] Ember Observer provides a directory of addons stored in npm, but goes a step further by scoring these addons to rank the health and maturity of the addon. These metrics tell you whether the addon is open source; the quality of the code, tests, and documentation; the quality of the addon's continuous integration practices; whether the addon is actively maintained; and the popularity of the addon on GitHub. Once you've found the addon you want to use, the README.md file usually tells you how to use the project.

There's a lot of productivity to be gained from using addons, but sometimes you have a great idea that you want to share with others. For that, you may want to develop your own addon. Developing an addon and learning how to release it to the community is the last step on our journey.

## Develop Your Own Addon

If you work with Ember and Ember CLI long enough, you'll find that you want to share code between apps, whether pointing multiple apps at an addon in a private Git repository, or publishing your addon publicly via npm. We've already seen how to obtain and use a third-party addon within your app. Now, let's talk about how to create an addon to be shared between your applications, or even to be used by others.

A natural use of Ember addons is to create a reusable web component library. Many such libraries exist that contain reusable web controls, like buttons or menu bars; we've even discussed a few in this book. Let's start a small one right now with a single control: a Bootstrap-styled drop-down list, which we'll use to replace the notebook list in the EmberNote app with a drop-down of notebook records. This drop-down will change to the chosen notebook when the user picks an entry in the list.

We'll start by creating the basic structure for our addon using Ember CLI.

### Creating the Addon

When you create an addon, you're not creating a class that's part of an existing app. You're actually creating an entirely new codebase. So, for the

---

1.  emberobserver.com

first time since Chapter 1, we're going to leave the ember-note directory tree and create a new directory structure for this addon. First, navigate to the parent of your ember-note directory. Then, run the following command as a user with admin privileges, which will create a new directory:

```
$ ember addon ember-bs-dropdown
```

Just like when you created EmberNote, this command creates the full directory structure for your addon. We'll go over the most important parts of this structure as we work on the addon.

Because we're going to create a Bootstrap-styled drop-down, our addon needs the Bootstrap stylesheet. Change to the newly created addon directory and install Bootstrap.

```
$ cd ember-bs-dropdown
$ bower install bootstrap --save
```

Because we installed Bootstrap earlier, the bower install command checks the local cache for Bootstrap. Most likely it will find Bootstrap in the cache, but we still need to run this command because it also adds Bootstrap to the addon as a dependency. The bower install command does this by editing the addon's bower.json file to include Bootstrap.

Now that your project has Bootstrap, we're ready to generate our component. Run the following command:

```
$ ember generate component bs-dropdown --pod
```

This should all be familiar to you. So far, the biggest difference between creating an addon and an app is just the initial command: ember new for an app; ember addon for an addon.

If you look at the directory structure for the addon, it's familiar, too, with one exception: there's an addon directory at the top level, the same level as the app directory.

This can seem confusing at first, but there's a good reason for it. When you include an addon in an Ember app, the addon code is placed in your app's node_modules directory. However, like with anything else, you might want to extend the addon module. The files in the app directory become part of your app's namespace, and can be extended by your app, as shown in the following figure.

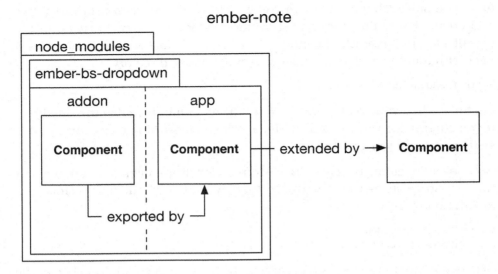

Previously when we ran the command ember generate component bs-dropdown --pod, it generated three files. Two of these are the component.js and template.hbs files that are generated with a standard component. Let's look at these files.

First, the generated component looks like this:

```
ch9/ember-bs-dropdown/addon/components/bs-dropdown/component.js
import Ember from 'ember';
import layout from './template';

export default Ember.Component.extend({
  layout: layout
});
```

We don't need to make any changes to the generated code because we're not going to build a very sophisticated component. Our goal is just to build a drop-down that we can use to navigate to the notes route. So this is all we need. The previous class simply instantiates a component. Our template is a bit more detailed:

```
ch9/ember-bs-dropdown/addon/components/bs-dropdown/template.hbs
<div class="dropdown">
  <button class="btn btn-default dropdown-toggle" type="button"
    id="dropdownMenu1" data-toggle="dropdown" aria-haspopup="true"
    aria-expanded="true">
      {{dropdownName}}
      <span class="caret"></span>
  </button>
  <ul class="dropdown-menu" aria-labelledby="dropdownMenu1">
    {{#each model as |list|}}
```

```
      <li>{{#link-to route list.id}}{{list.title}}{{/link-to}}</li>
    {{/each}}
  </ul>
</div>
{{yield}}
```

Much of this code is boilerplate Bootstrap for creating a drop-down. The {{dropdownName}} expression is used to pass a value to the component, which will be used as the default display value for the drop-down. The {{each}} expression loops along the passed-in model of items to display. Each item becomes a single line in the drop-down.

Each line in the drop-down consists of the {{link-to}} expression. We rely on three pieces of data in building these expressions. First, we pass in the name of the destination route so we know where to go when we pick a notebook. Then, we use the id value of the current record in the list as the parameter value to pass to the destination route, and the title of the record to use as the display value in the drop-down. We'll see how to use this from our app shortly.

Let's take a quick look now at the class created in our app directory.

`ch9/ember-bs-dropdown/app/components/bs-dropdown/component.js`
```
export { default } from 'ember-bs-dropdown/components/bs-dropdown/component';
```

That's right—it's a single line of code. It's not the clearest code, but what it does is helpful. This single line of code creates an extensible version of the addon's component class, and makes that version a part of your app's namespace. Your app doesn't get a copy of the file, but you can extend this class in your app to add your own functionality onto the component, such as providing default values for a component's variables.

That's all the code we need to develop the addon. We'll need to do a few more things to make it usable. First, we need to tell Ember CLI to use the HTMLBars compiler when it builds the addon for use elsewhere. Run the following from the project root, which installs ember-cli-htmlbars as a dependency of the project:

```
$ npm install ember-cli-htmlbars --save
```

We also need to make sure that the addon is built with a copy of the Bootstrap files it needs. We're not going to use the ember-cli-build.js file to do this, however. Each app has only one ember-cli-build.js, so even if we added the Bootstrap assets to the addon's ember-cli-build.js, when the app includes our addon it will ignore the addon's ember-cli-build.js and use its own. Instead, we add these assets in the addon's entry point, index.js:

ch9/ember-bs-dropdown/index.js
```
/* jshint node: true */
'use strict';

module.exports = {
  name: 'ember-bs-dropdown',

  included: function(app) {
    app.import('bower_components/bootstrap/dist/css/bootstrap.css');
    app.import('bower_components/bootstrap/dist/css/bootstrap.css.map',{
      destDir: 'assets'
    });
    app.import('bower_components/bootstrap/dist/js/bootstrap.min.js');
  }
};
```

The *entry point* is a npm concept. An entry point is code that your package, in this case your Ember addon, includes in another resource. The entry point code will be run when the containing resource is first run in a browser. As you can see, we are doing much the same work with this entry point as we do in the app's ember-cli-build.js, except that we also include some Bootstrap JavaScript to allow our new drop-down to work properly. When the calling app includes this addon, the included function will execute, and the Bootstrap assets will become part of the calling app.

Now that we've seen how to create a basic addon, let's learn how we can use it in a local application to test it out.

## Using the Addon

The addon is now ready to be used in the EmberNote app. First, we need to make the addon visible to EmberNote. While using your local environment for both the ember-bs-dropdown addon and the EmberNote app, you can use a set of npm commands to make the addon package available locally. We'll see how to publish addons to npm or a private repository in *Publishing Your Addon*, on page 128.

To make your local npm cache aware of the addon, run the following command from the ember-bs-dropdown directory:

```
$ npm link
```

This command creates a symbolic link from the local npm cache to your addon project. This link allows other projects on your local machine to use your addon, with one additional step. Your local app needs to also create a link to the Ember addon. So, from the ember-note directory, run the following command:

```
$ npm link ember-bs-dropdown
```

The EmberNote app is now able to locate the addon we've created. However, while we've given the app a path to see the addon, it's still not aware of it. If you have a running instance of ember serve, stop it now. Then, add the following line to the very bottom of the devDependencies section of the EmberNote package.json file, which is in the root directory (be sure to add a comma to the end of the preceding line):

```
"ember-bs-dropdown": "*"
```

Now, when we next run ember serve, the app will see the drop-down component. Don't try it just yet; we have one more change to make to the EmberNote app first. Open the notebooks template and modify it to look like the following:

```
ch9/ember-note/app/notebooks/template.hbs
<div>
  <div class="col-md-3">
    <div>Notebooks</div>
    <div>
      title: {{input value=title}}
      <button {{action 'addNotebook'}}>Add</button>
    </div>
    {{bs-dropdown model=model route='notebooks.notes'
      dropdownName='Notebooks'}}
  </div>
  <div class="col-md-9">
    {{outlet}}
  </div>
</div>
```

We've switched out a great deal of code for our new addon component. We use the {{bs-dropdown}} expression to refer to our custom component. The model=model portion of the expression passes the notebooks model into the component. Because this model class contains the right properties, namely the id and title properties, it should work just fine. We pass the notebooks.notes route name as the destination route for the drop-down, and "Notebooks" as the default drop-down value.

Before this will work, we need to make one last change to the app. We need to remove the Bootstrap assets from our ember-cli-build.js. If we leave them in, the ember serve command complains that we've defined them twice. Because we're now relying on a Bootstrap-derived addon for our components, we'll let it define the version we use. Change the ember-cli-build.js file to look like this:

```
ch9/ember-note/ember-cli-build.js
/* global require, module */
var EmberApp = require('ember-cli/lib/broccoli/ember-app');

module.exports = function(defaults) {
```

```
var app = new EmberApp(defaults, {
  // Add options here
});

// Use `app.import` to add additional libraries to the generated
// output files.
//
// If you need to use different assets in different
// environments, specify an object as the first parameter. That
// object's keys should be the environment name and the values
// should be the asset to use in that environment.
//
// If the library that you are including contains AMD or ES6
// modules that you would like to import into your application
// please specify an object with the list of modules as keys
// along with the exports of each module as its value.

  return app.toTree();
};
```

This file now looks just like it did when we started the book. From a command line, run ember serve and you should see that our drop-down is in use. You can use it to choose the notebook you wish to review, and the related notes will be loaded into the notes route.

Ember CLI offers a number of other ways to test your addon. It provides a dummy app within the addon project (under tests/dummy), as well as the ability to write test cases with QUnit. I chose to focus on using the EmberNote app for testing, but when you're building a real addon, you'll want to rely on those as well.

Now that you have an addon ready to share, how do you get it out into the world? The last stop on our journey is one where we'll learn to give back to others who have helped pave the path for us. Let's learn how to publish an addon and share it with the world.

## Publishing Your Addon

So you've made something cool, and you're very proud of it. So proud that you think others might benefit from using it as well, either within your company or out in the world at large. Let's learn now how to share our addon code with the world.

### Publishing Privately

Sometimes you make something cool, but it's proprietary. For whatever reason, you can't totally open-source your addon. But you also want to make sure that multiple apps can benefit. Luckily, you can publish an addon to a private repository.

Ember CLI supports the use of privately published addons with a single command. Just store your addon code in a Git repository, and you can simply run the ember install command using the repository's URL as the addon name. Your addon will be installed into your project, and you can continue to use it just as if it were published publicly.

### Publishing to npm

Of course, the fame, glory, and riches of publishing a hit open source Ember addon might be too enticing to pass up. If that's the case, you can publish your addon to npm.

When you created your addon, Ember CLI created a package.json file. Contained within that file are the two attributes required to publish your package: name and version. That's all you need.

Before you can publish it, you need to be registered with npm. If you haven't already done so, run npm adduser to add a user to the npmjs.com site. Once you've logged in as this user, you can then run npm publish to publish your new addon, and it will be publicly available via the npm site.

When you're ready to release a new version, you can bump the version number using npm version, and provide an update_type of either patch, minor, or major, depending on the nature of your change.

Once your addon package is published, other developers can access it via the ember install command, just like they would any other addon. And you can be happy that you've given a little something back to the community.

## Next Steps

We've come to the end of our road together, and there's still plenty to be learned. Before we part ways, here are a few suggestions on what you can do next to continue working with Ember and supporting the community.

There are many ways to support the Ember community, including contributing to the core framework or writing online about your use of Ember. These are strongly encouraged. However, the ability to share code that others might find useful via Ember addons is another great way to give back.

Ember is a mature framework in many ways, and it offers a lot of great features out of the box. However, there are many features that might be useful to a lot of developers without belonging in the core framework. That's why one of the most compelling features of the Ember ecosystem is the Ember addon.

There's also much more to Ember than we were able to cover here. The Ember team does a great job of maintaining the project's documentation. If you run across a use case that we haven't discussed, there's a good chance that Ember accounts for it, or there's an addon that does. So check the docs on the Ember site or Ember Observer!

The Ember project is always moving forward, and there are a number of great features in process at any time that will no doubt be useful to you. I'll make every effort to keep this book fresh, but I encourage also you to check out the following sources to keep up with the project:

- The Ember site: emberjs.com

- Ember on GitHub: github.com/emberjs

- Ember CLI: www.ember-cli.com

- Ember Weekly: emberweekly.com

- Ember Observer: emberobserver.com

Last, I want to thank you for taking the time to read this book. I hope you've found it helpful. If you have any comments or concerns, please share them via the forum at forums.pragprog.com/forums/368 or on the errata page at pragprog.com/titles/mwjsember/errata. Happy programming!

# Index

## SYMBOLS

() => (fat arrow function), 11
{{ }} (Handlebars expression syntax), 9

## A

abstraction
    mixins, 91, 94–96
    sharing services with dependency injection, 98–102
    transforms, 102
    utilities, 91–94
acceptance testing, 115–116
{{action}} expression
    binding actions to routes, 46
    login route, 21
    register route, 10
action property, 44
actions
    {{input}} expression, 44
    binding, 44–45
    handling with components, 54, 57–61
    placeholders, 60
    scope, 56, 58
    sent actions, 58–61
actions hash
    building register route, 11
    components, 58
    login route, 22–23
    notebooks route, 29
adapter type, 79
adapters, see also RESTAdapter class
    about, 66

adapter/serializer pattern, 89
    injection, 79
    model-specific, 89
addNew, 10–11, 96
addNotebook, 83
addon command, 122
addons, 121–130
    {{content-for}} expressions, 7
    creating, 122–126
    defined, 16, 55
    developing, 122–128
    Ember CLI Datepicker, 47
    Ember CLI Materialize, 61
    Ember CLI Simple Auth, 80
    Ember Inspector, 117–118
    ember-cli-htmlbars, 37, 125
    ember-cli-showdown, 55, 121
    Fireplace, 75
    Handlebars, 37
    installing, 121
    markdown-to-html, 55, 114
    publishing, 128–129
    resources, 47, 122
    testing, 128
    validations, 97
administrative user, installing as, 2
after, 99
afterEach, 117
andThen, 117
anonymous declaration, 22

APIs, nonstandard, 77–89, see also RESTful services
    accessing with serializers, 82–85
    adding custom hostname, 81
    modifying data in flight, 87–89
    querying, 85
    request headers, 78–81
App class, 8
app.js, 6–7
application object, 79
application route, 9, 19
application.hbs
    about, 9
    creating, 6
    login route, 20, 23
    single-page applications, 35–38
ArrayController, 42
attr function, 64
authentication
    Ember CLI Simple Auth, 80
    nonstandard APIs, 78–81
    random number generation, 112
autofocus property, 45

## B

before, 99
beforeEach, 117
belongsTo, 64
binding
    actions, 44–45

click events, 10
input fields, 43–45
block expressions, 42, 56
blueprints, 106, 115
body-parser library, 13
BooleanTransform, 64, 103
Bootstrap
addon example of drop-down list, 122–128
installing stylesheets, 3
bound variables, 44
Bower
Bootstrap, 123
installing, 2, 106, 123
as prerequisite, 1
upgrades, 106
browser-based caching, 68–75
{{bs-dropdown}} expression, 127
BSD, installing as administrative user, 2
build command, 119
build system, 105–107, 119, 125
buttons
adding id parameter, 113
binding actions, 10, 46

## C

caching
browser-based, 68–75
npm and addons, 126
case
converting, 83
querying nonconventional APIs, 85
chaining conditions, 42
checkbox property, 45
checked property, 45
classes, injecting, 99–102
click events
binding, 10
components, 60, 114
close action, 51, 60
closeNote, 59, 112–115
closing tags, block expressions, 42
code
for this book, xi
reusing in Ember, 91–104
cols property, 45
command-line interface, see Ember CLI

compiling templates, 46
component.js
addons, 124
edit-note directory, 52
component.set, 114
components, 49–61
action handling, 54, 57–61
addon example, 122–128
altering root element, 56
creating, 50–52
custom elements, 54
defined, 49
event listening, 60
files for, 52
integrating with {{yield}} expression, 54, 56
nesting, 55–56
reusing with, 49–61
scope, 56, 58
sent actions, 59–61
templates and, 35, 50, 52, 59
unit testing, 112–115
user interface, 53–57
computed properties, 81
conditionals, template, 42
container, 79
Container tab, Ember Inspector, 118
{{content-for}} expression, 7
context, action handling, 57
continuous integration, 107
controller parameter for rendering, 33
controllers
avoiding, 10–11
deprecation, 11
model hooks, 29
rendering data, 41
rendering into named outlets, 33
controls
addons, 47
rendering with Handlebars expressions, 41–46
segmenting into templates, 38–41
convention-over-configuration, 4, 77, 91
converting
case, 83
currency, 103

data in flight, 87–89
model names from payload root, 86
copying mock server files, 77
create, 100
createRecord, 11, 71
CSS, see also stylesheets
Materialize addon, 61
template component, 35
Ctrl-C
pausing test output, 107
quitting app, 15
curly brackets ({{ }}) Handlebars expression syntax, 9
currency conversion, 103
custom API hostname, adding, 81
custom elements, 54

## D

dashes, naming conventions, 52, 92
data
adding data service, 12–16, 25–30
deleting, 73
getting from containing templates, 52
loading from RESTful services, 65–70
modeling, 63–76
modifying in flight, 87–89
nonstandard APIs, 77–89
normalizing, 84
purging, 75
querying RESTful services, 66–68
querying nonstandard APIs, 85
rendering with Handlebars expressions, 41
saving records, 71, 74
serializing from nonstandard APIs, 82–85
transforms, 102
updating records, 72
validation examples, 92, 94
working with records, 70–75, 125
data services, adding, 16
Data tab, Ember Inspector, 118
datastores, NEDB project, 13, 77
Datepicker addon, 47

DateTransform, 64, 103

debugging, 117–118

deleteRecord, 73

deleting
    adapters and serializers, 89
    data from unconventional APIs, 88
    records, 73

dependencies
    dependency injection, 58, 78–81, 98–102
    deploying apps, 119
    ECMAScript 2015, 7
    management, 105
    saving as dev-only, 13, 106
    updating, 106

dependency injection
    components, 58
    defined, 98
    limiting, 101
    sharing services, 98–102
    user session, 78–81

deployment, 5, 106, 119

Deprecations tab, Ember Inspector, 118

deserialization, 104

destoryRecord, 74

destroy, 89

developer ergonomics, 1

development version of build, 119

direct object reference vulnerability, 25

directories
    addons, 122
    creating, 3, 5, 122
    structure, 4

dirty objects, 75

disabled property, 45

<div> tag as root element, 56

Dockyard, 97

documentation
    addons, 121
    Ember, 130

DOM
    custom elements, 54
    Handlebars expressions, 9
    single-page applications, 35
    template compilers, 46

drop-down list addon example, 122–128

{{dropdownName}} expression, 125

DS.Store object, 65, 68–75

dummy app, 128

E

{{#each}} expression
    ArrayController, 42
    drop-down list addon, 125
    notebooks route, 29
    template hierarchy, 39–41

ECMA International, 7

ECMAScript 2015, 7, 11, 22–23

edit-note, 52–57, 112–115

{{else}} segment, 39

email, validation, 94–96

Ember, see also Ember CLI
    advantages, ix
    documentation, 130
    Handlebars and, 37
    installing, 1–2
    validations addon, 97

Ember CLI, see also addons
    abstracting functions with utilities, 91–94
    adding data service, 12–16
    application template, 35–38
    build system, 105–107, 119, 125
    building register route, 10–12
    dependency management, 105
    deployment, 5, 106, 119
    ECMAScript 2015, 7
    HTTP mocks, 13–16, 27
    installing, 1–2, 106
    new app setup, 3–5
    prerequisites, 1
    race condition, 3
    registering users, 5–10
    reusing components, 49–61
    routes, 17–34
    testing, 107–118, 128

Ember CLI Datepicker, 47

Ember CLI Materialize, 61

Ember CLI Mirage, 16

Ember CLI Simple Auth, 80

Ember Data, see also data
    about, 63
    adding data service, 12–16
    creating new model object, 11
    dependency injection, 101
    loading records, 51
    model hooks, 24
    modeling, 63–76
    modifying data in flight, 87–89
    monitoring request/response traffic, 71
    nonstandard APIs, 77–89
    notebooks route, 29
    path names, 86
    RESTful call conventions, 82
    serializers, 82–85
    as service, 98
    transforms, 102

Ember Observer, 122, 130

Ember Simple Auth, 80

Ember Weekly, 130

ember-cli-build.js, 125

ember-cli-htmlbars, 125

ember-cli-showdown, 55, 121

ember-note.css, 7

ember-note.js, 7, 36

ember-qunit, 109

ember-test-helpers, 109

EmberNote
    about, xi
    adding data service, 12–16
    building app, 105–107
    building register route, 10–12
    creating notes, 50–52
    creating repository, 3
    data validation examples, 92, 94
    defining routes, 19–23
    deployment, 119
    drop-down list, 122–128
    login route, 18–23, 79
    model hook, 23–30, 51
    modeling data, 63–76
    nonstandard APIs, 77–82
    registering users, 5–10
    reusing code, 91–104
    reusing components, 49–61
    route structure, 17–34
    Router class, 17–19

running, 4, 107
setup, 3–5
testing, 107–118
user interface templates,
35–47
user interface with components, 53–57
endpoint
adapting to path name
variations, 86
login route, 22
nonstandard APIs, 78,
82–83
enter, binding actions, 44
entry point, 126
--environment production flag, 119
ergonomics, developer, 1
errors
debugging, 117–118
repository creation, 3
unit testing, 111
ES 2015, *see* ECMAScript
2015
ES6, *see* ECMAScript 2015
escape-press, binding actions,
44
event handlers, *see* actions
event listening, components,
60
Evernote, xi, 3, *see also* EmberNote
execution order
initializers, 99
tests, 107
extractArray, 88
extractSingle, 88

**F**

factories, injecting classes,
100
FastBoot, 46
fat arrow function (() =>), 11
fields
binding input, 43–45
defining model, 63
find, 67
findAll, 68–69
findQuery, 86
findRecord, 69
Firebase, 75
Fireplace, 75
fixtures, 12
focus-in, binding actions, 44

focus-out, binding actions, 44
folder structure, creating, 4
foo example of limited dependency injection, 101
form property, 45
format validation option, 97
functions, abstracting with
utilities, 91–94

**G**

-g flag, 2, 106
generate
about, 5
--pod flag, 5
GET, 68
get endpoint, 22
getRandomValues(), 112
Git
installing, 2
publishing addons, 129
GitHub, ix, 130
global installation flag, 2, 106
Google's Material Design
spec, 61

**H**

Handlebars
about, x, 37
components, 52–53
rendering controls, 41–46
templates, 9, 35, 37
hasChrome, 43
hasDirtyAttributes, 75
hasMany, 64
hash, defined, 11
headers, nonstandard APIs, 78–
81
hostname, adding custom
API, 81
HTML, *see also* components;
Handlebars; Markdown
attributes, 44
binding input fields, 43–
45
properties, 45
rendering controls with
Handlebars expres-
sions, 41–46
as template component,
9, 35, 37
HTMLBars, 37, 46, 125, *see
also* Handlebars

HTTP
Ember CLI HTTP mocks,
13–16, 27
parsing, 13
request headers for non-
standard APIs, 78–81

**I**

IDs
acceptance tests, 116
API endpoints, 83
buttons, 113
drop-down list addon,
125
passing note, 50
querying RESTful ser-
vices, 67
{{#if}} expression, 20, 22, 42
if shortcut, 43
import
unit tests, 109, 111
utility functions, 93
inFlight state, 74
includeId attribute, 83
included function, 126
inclusion validation option, 97
indeterminate property, 45
index.html
about, 6
creating, 6
EmberNote, 35–38
init command, 106
initialize function, 79, 98, 100
initializers
dependency injection, 98–
102
diagram, 101
logger, 99
user sessions from non-
standard APIs, 78
inject, 79, 100
{{input}} expression
binding input fields, 43–
45
edit-note template, 54
HTML attributes list, 44
login route, 21
register route, 10
input fields, binding, 43–45
insert-newline, binding actions,
44
installation
addons, 121
as administrative user, 2
Bootstrap, 123

Bower, 2, 106, 123
Ember and Ember CLI,
1–2, 106
ember-cli-htmlbars, 125
global flag, 2, 106
Node, npm and Git, 2
PhantomJS, 2
validations addon, 97
watchman, 3
instantiate property, 100
integration, continuous, 107
into parameter for rendering,
33
isValid, 97
isValidEmail, 94–96
isValidLength, 94

J

JavaScript, *see also* PhantomJS; QUnit
components, 52
deploying apps, 119
ECMAScript 2015, 7
Firebase, 75
Handlebars, 37
Node, 1
JSON
changing payload root, 86
serializing data, 83
validations addon, 97

K

key-press, binding actions, 44
key-value pairs
model fields, 64, 71
querying nonconventional
APIs, 86

L

legacy APIs, accessing with
serializers, 82–85
library component, addon example, 122–128
link command, 126
{{#link-to}} expression
drop-down list addon,
125
login route, 21, 23
nested templates, 39–41
notes, 51
register route, 9
links
addons and npm cache,
126
creating, 9
login route, 21, 23

nested templates, 39–41
notes, 51
Linux, installing as administrative user, 2
listing
addon example of drop-
down list, 122–128
notebooks, 28–29
literals, transitioning between
routes, 33
loading
data from RESTful ser-
vices, 65–70
notes, 51
local deployment, 106
logger initializer, 99–102
logger property, 101
login action, 22
login route, 18–23, 79
login template, 21
looping, template, 42

M

major addon update type, 129
map, 8
Markdown
about, xi, 49
installing addon, 55, 121
unit testing, 114
markdown attribute, 55
markdown-to-html addon, 55, 114
{{markdown-to-html}} expression,
55
Material Design spec,
Google's, 61
Materialize CSS, 61
Math.random function, 111–112
{{message}} expression, 10
minor addon update type, 129
mixins, 91, 94–97
mock objects, unit testing
components, 114
mock services
adding, 12–16, 25–30
adding data service, 16
copying files, 77
Ember CLI HTTP mocks,
13–16, 27
model hook
querying RESTful ser-
vices, 67
reusing components, 51

transitioning between
routes, 33
using, 23–30
model objects, creating, 11
model parameter for rendering,
33
model property, 53
model=model expression, 127
modelNameFromPayloadKey, 86–87
models, 63–76
creating, 12, 26, 28
defining fields, 63
defining relationships,
64–65
loading data from REST-
ful services, 65–70
model property, 53
model-specific adapters
and serializers, 89
model=model expression,
127
name from payload root,
86
rendering into named
outlets, 33
transitioning between
routes, 33
unit testing, 110–112
moduleForComponent, 114
moduleForModel, 109
modulePrefix, 8
modules
about, 3
App class as, 8
testing, 108
Mustache, 37

N

name attribute, 99
name property, 45
named outlets, 33, 37
named-parameter queries, 70
names
adapting to path name
variations, 86
custom API hostnames,
81
initializers, 99
injecting factories, 100
name property, 45
naming conventions, 52,
92
from payload root, 86
NEDB project, 13, 77

nesting
    components, 55–56
    routes, 30–32
    templates, 39–41
new, 3, 6
Node
    about, x, 1
    installing, 2
    NEDB project, 13
node instance, 4
node_modules directory, 121, 123
NodeWatcher, 3
normalize, 84
normalizeHash, 85
normalizing data, 84
note model, unit testing, 108–115
note object, mock service, 27
note template, 53
note-test.js, 108
note.id value, 51
note=model assignment, 53
noteCount function, 110–112
notebook model
    defining model relationships, 64–65
    developing addon example, 122–128
    querying nonconventional APIs, 85
notebooks
    creating, 28
    creating notes, 50–52
    creating records, 70
    creating route, 18–23
    defining model relationships, 64–65
    developing addon example, 122–128
    listing, 28–29
    model hook, 23–30
    modifying data in flight, 87–89
    nesting routes, 30–32
    querying nonconventional APIs, 85
    redirecting to, 22
    serializing data, 82
    templates, 28, 38–41, 43
    test case dependencies, 109
    unit testing, 110–115
notebooks route
    creating, 18–23

creating records, 70
model hook, 23–30
redirecting to, 22
serializers, 82
unit testing, 110–115
notebooks template
    binding input fields, 43
    contents, 38
    hierarchy, 39–41
notes
    creating, 50–52
    defining model relationships, 64–65
    modifying data in flight, 87–89
    nested routes, 32
    saving, 58, 112–115
    title validation examples, 92, 94
    unit testing, 108–115
notes route
    creating, 50, 53
    missing route, 32
    mixins, 95
    nested routes, 31
    validation utility example, 92
npm
    about, x
    addons, 16, 121, 126, 129
    entry point, 126
    installing, 2
    upgrades, 106
npm version, 129
numbers, random, 111–112
NumberTransform, 64, 103

**O**
OAuth, 80
object-oriented design, ix
ObjectController, 42
opening tags, block expressions, 42
options
    injecting classes, 100
    nonstandard APIs, 83
    rendering, 33
OS X, installing as administrative user, 2
{{outlet}} expression
    login route, 21, 23
    registered users, 9
    rendering into named outlets, 33, 37

templates, 37
transitioning between routes, 33
outlet parameter for rendering, 33

**P**
package.json file, addons, 127, 129
params object, model hooks, 24
parsing HTTP, 13
patch addon update type, 129
path
    adapting to name variations, 86
    addons, 127
    passing note ID, 51
    segments and route definition, 24
    segments and security, 25
path attribute, 51
pathForType method, 86
pattern variable, 95
payload, changing root, 86
payload method parameter, 88
peekAll, 69
PhantomJS, 1–2, 107
placeholders, action, 60
--pod flag, 5, 19, 24, 38, 53
podModulePrefix, 8
POST, 13, 71
production, deploying to, 119
Promises, 22–23, 71
properties
    adding with mixins, 97
    computed, 81
    records, 71
property function, 81
publishing addons, 128
purging records, 75
PUT, 71–72

**Q**
querying
    nonstandard APIs, 85
    RESTful services, 66–68
quitting app, 15
QUnit, 109, 128
quotes, 43–44

# R

race conditions, 3
random function, 111–112
random number generation, 111–112
records, *see also* data
creating, 70
deleting, 73
drop-down list addon, 125
modifying with store object, 68
purging, 75
saving, 11, 71, 74
state, 74–75
updating, 72
working with, 70–75
refreshing lists, 30
register directory, 5
register method, 79, 100
register route
acceptance testing, 116
building, 10–12
creating, 8
links, 9
mixins, 96
register.js, creating, 6
registering
injected classes, 100, 102
limited dependency injection, 101
with npm, 129
user sessions, 79
users, 5–10
regular expressions, 95, 97
reload, 69
reloading
lists, 29
records, 69
render, 33
rendering
data, 41
into named outlets, 33
server-side, 46
repositories
creating, 3
publishing addons, 128
race condition, 3
request headers for nonstandard APIs, 78–81
request/response traffic, monitoring, 71
Resolver, 8
resources
addons, 47, 122

for this book, ix, xi, 2
components, 54
Ember and Ember CLI, 130
Ember CLI Materialize, 61
Ember CLI Mirage, 16
Ember CLI Simple Auth, 80
events, 61
Handlebars, 37
RSVP, 23
validations addon, 97
RESTAdapter
adding custom API hostname, 81
creating, 12–13
loading data, 66
nonstandard APIs, 78–82
path name variations, 86
querying nonconventional APIs, 85
request headers for nonstandard APIs, 78
user session, 80
RESTAdapter class, 130
RESTful services
about, 66, 82
adding, 12–16, 25–30
loading data from, 65–70
modeling data, 63–76
querying, 66–68
saving records, 71
using store, 68
working with records, 70–75
RESTSerializer
accessing legacy APIs, 82–85
changing payload root, 86
creating, 12
modifying data in flight, 87–89
RESTSerializer class, 130
Return key, binding actions, 44
reusing
code, 91–104
components, 49–61
rollbackAttributes, 75
root HTML element, 56
root URL, 19, 66
root key, 86
root route, 9
Route class
application route, 19

defined, 17
dependency injection, 101
ECMAScript 2015, 22
route directory, 6
route type, injecting into, 79
route.js
defining empty route classes, 10
login route, 20
nested routes, 32
note route, 53
--pod flag, 5, 24
Router class
creating components, 50
defining app structure, 8
hierarchy diagram, 17
organizing app, 17–19
path segments, 24
as service, 98
router.js
about, 8
creating, 6
creating components, 50
defining routes, 19, 23
hierarchy of routes, 6
nested routes, 30
routes, 17–34
acceptance testing, 115–116
adding, 18
binding actions to, 45
building register route, 10–12
components, 50
controllers, 41
creating, 5
defined, 5, 8, 17
defining, 10, 19–23
hierarchy, 6, 9, 17
injection, 79
mixins, 95
model hook, 23–30, 51
moving between, 23, 32
nesting, 30–33
organizing app, 17–19
path segments, 24
root, 9
templates and, 9, 19, 38
uses, 10
validation utility example, 92
rows property, 45
RSVP, 23

run loop, unit testing, 111, 114

running app with serve command, 4, 107

## S

save, 11, 58, 71, 114

--save-dev flag, 13, 106

saveNote, 58, 112–115

saved state, 74

saving
    apps, 5
    dev-only dependencies, 13, 106
    notes, 58, 112–115
    records, 11, 71, 74

scope
    actions, 56, 58
    templates, 56

security
    path segments, 25
    random number generation, 112

sendAction, 59

sent actions, 58–61

serialize method, 83

serializers, *see also* RESTSerializer class
    accessing legacy APIs, 82–85
    adapter/serializer pattern, 89
    defined, 82
    model-specific, 89
    test case dependencies, 109
    transforms, 104

serve, 4, 107

server-side rendering, 46

services, *see also* RESTful services
    defined, 98
    sharing with dependency injection, 98–102

Session, creating and using from nonstandard APIs, 78–81

session management, Ember CLI Simple Auth, 80

session variable, 79

setup, new app, 3–5

sharing services with dependency injection, 98–102

side effects, unit testing, 114

Simple Auth addon, 80

single-page applications, 35–38

singleton property, 100

snapshot parameter, 83

speed, server-side rendering, 46

state
    mixins, 94–95
    records, 74–75
    user interface, 10

storage
    data services, 12–16
    NEDB project, 13, 77
    store object, 65, 67

store object, 65, 67–75

strings
    model field type, 64
    quotes, 43
    sendAction, 59

stubs, *see* mock services

stylesheets
    Bootstrap, 3, 123
    deploying apps, 119
    index.html, 7
    Materialize addon, 61
    template component, 35

sudo, 2

## T

tabindex property, 45

targetObject, 115

template.hbs
    addons, 124
    edit-note directory, 52
    login route, 20, 23
    nested routes, 32
    note route, 53
    notebooks route, 29
    --pod flag, 5, 38

templates
    application, 6, 9, 20, 23, 35–38
    compiling, 46
    components and, 35, 50, 52, 59
    creating, 38
    defined, 9
    getting data from containing, 52
    hierarchy, 36, 39–41
    linking, 39–41
    login route, 21
    looping and conditionals, 42
    nested routes, 32

notebooks, 38–41, 43

notebooks route, 28

reloading, 29

rendering into named outlets, 33, 37

routes and, 9, 19, 38

scope, 56

segmenting UI into, 38–41

user interface, 35–47

templates directory, 38

templates folder, 19

test runner, unit testing, 111

testing, 107–118
    acceptance tests, 115–116
    addons, 128
    debugging, 117–118
    test execution, 107
    test frameworks, 109
    unit tests, 108–115
    viewing tests, 107

{{textarea}} expression, 45, 54

then, 71

this
    fat arrow function (() =>), 11
    mixins, 95

this._super, 85

this.subject, 111

titles
    data validation examples, 92, 94
    drop-down list addon, 125

traffic, monitoring, 71

Transform, 64, 102

transforms, 64, 102

transitionTo, 22, 32

types, model field, 64

## U

unbound variables, 44

uncommitted state, 74

unit testing, 108–115

{{#unless}} expression
    controlling templates with conditionals, 43
    login route, 21–22

unloadAll, 70

unloadRecord, 75

update_type, 129

updating
    dependencies, 106

lists, 29
published addons, 129
records, 72
upgrading Ember and Ember CLI, 105
URLs
acceptance testing, 117
altering Ember Data, 68
nested templates, 40–41
publishing addons, 129
relation to application location, 40
root, 19, 66
routes, 5, 19
user attribute, 20, 22
user interface, 35–47
components, 53–57
registration, 10
rendering controls with Handlebars expressions, 41–46
segmenting into templates, 38–41

single-page applications, 35–38
state, 10
user_id, path segments, 24
users
creating user session from nonstandard APIs, 78–81
login, 18–23, 79
registering, 5–10
utilities, abstracting, 91–94

V
validation
data, 92, 94
email, 94–96
validations addon, 97
validations property, 97
values
bound vs. unbound variables, 44
Promises, 22–23
validation, 96

variables, bound vs. unbound, 44
vendor.css, 7
vendor.js, 7
versions
Ember and Ember CLI, 105
Node, 2
publishing addons, 129
template compilers, 46
views, event listening, 60

W
W3C specifications for custom elements, 54
watchman, 3, 107
WebSockets, 107
Windows, installing as administrative user, 2

Y
{{yield}} expression, 54, 56

# The Modern Web

Get up to speed on the latest HTML, CSS, and JavaScript techniques.

## HTML5 and CSS3 (2nd edition)

HTML5 and CSS3 are more than just buzzwords—
they're the foundation for today's web applications.
This book gets you up to speed on the HTML5 elements
and CSS3 features you can use right now in your current projects, with backwards compatible solutions
that ensure that you don't leave users of older browsers
behind. This new edition covers even more new features, including CSS animations, IndexedDB, and
client-side validations.

Brian P. Hogan
(314 pages) ISBN: 9781937785598. $38
*https://pragprog.com/book/bhh52e*

## Async JavaScript

With the advent of HTML5, front-end MVC, and
Node.js, JavaScript is ubiquitous—and still messy.
This book will give you a solid foundation for managing
async tasks without losing your sanity in a tangle of
callbacks. It's a fast-paced guide to the most essential
techniques for dealing with async behavior, including
PubSub, evented models, and Promises. With these
tricks up your sleeve, you'll be better prepared to
manage the complexity of large web apps and deliver
responsive code.

Trevor Burnham
(104 pages) ISBN: 9781937785277. $17
*https://pragprog.com/book/tbajs*

# The Joy of Math and Healthy Programming

Rediscover the joy and fascinating weirdness of pure mathematics, and learn how to take a healthier approach to programming.

## Good Math

Mathematics is beautiful—and it can be fun and exciting as well as practical. *Good Math* is your guide to some of the most intriguing topics from two thousand years of mathematics: from Egyptian fractions to Turing machines; from the real meaning of numbers to proof trees, group symmetry, and mechanical computation. If you've ever wondered what lay beyond the proofs you struggled to complete in high school geometry, or what limits the capabilities of the computer on your desk, this is the book for you.

Mark C. Chu-Carroll
(282 pages) ISBN: 9781937785338. $34
*https://pragprog.com/book/mcmath*

## The Healthy Programmer

To keep doing what you love, you need to maintain your own systems, not just the ones you write code for. Regular exercise and proper nutrition help you learn, remember, concentrate, and be creative—skills critical to doing your job well. Learn how to change your work habits, master exercises that make working at a computer more comfortable, and develop a plan to keep fit, healthy, and sharp for years to come.

*This book is intended only as an informative guide for those wishing to know more about health issues. In no way is this book intended to replace, countermand, or conflict with the advice given to you by your own healthcare provider including Physician, Nurse Practitioner, Physician Assistant, Registered Dietician, and other licensed professionals.*

Joe Kutner
(254 pages) ISBN: 9781937785314. $36
*https://pragprog.com/book/jkthp*

# The Pragmatic Bookshelf

The Pragmatic Bookshelf features books written by developers for developers. The titles continue the well-known Pragmatic Programmer style and continue to garner awards and rave reviews. As development gets more and more difficult, the Pragmatic Programmers will be there with more titles and products to help you stay on top of your game.

# Visit Us Online

### This Book's Home Page
*https://pragprog.com/book/mwjsember*
Source code from this book, errata, and other resources. Come give us feedback, too!

### Register for Updates
*https://pragprog.com/updates*
Be notified when updates and new books become available.

### Join the Community
*https://pragprog.com/community*
Read our weblogs, join our online discussions, participate in our mailing list, interact with our wiki, and benefit from the experience of other Pragmatic Programmers.

### New and Noteworthy
*https://pragprog.com/news*
Check out the latest pragmatic developments, new titles and other offerings.

# Save on the eBook

Save on the eBook versions of this title. Owning the paper version of this book entitles you to purchase the electronic versions at a terrific discount.

PDFs are great for carrying around on your laptop—they are hyperlinked, have color, and are fully searchable. Most titles are also available for the iPhone and iPod touch, Amazon Kindle, and other popular e-book readers.

Buy now at *https://pragprog.com/coupon*

# Contact Us

| | |
|---|---|
| Online Orders: | *https://pragprog.com/catalog* |
| Customer Service: | *support@pragprog.com* |
| International Rights: | *translations@pragprog.com* |
| Academic Use: | *academic@pragprog.com* |
| Write for Us: | *http://write-for-us.pragprog.com* |
| Or Call: | +1 800-699-7764 |

CPSIA information can be obtained
at www.ICGtesting.com
Printed in the USA
LVOW03s1531120416
483254LV00035B/239/P